LIVING WITHOUT FEAR
Dialogue with J. Krishnamurti

By the same author

THE GRAND DESIGN SERIES
(Volumes I-V)

A FREE SPIRIT

LIVING WITHOUT FEAR

Dialogue with J. Krishnamurti

by

Patrick Francis

Website:
www.geocities.com/granddesignie

Auricle Enterprises

Copyright © 2001 by Patrick Francis

Auricle Enterprises
30 Old Court Manor,
Firhouse
Dublin 24

Tel. (01) 4523793

All rights reserved. Other than for review purposes, no part of this book may be reproduced, stored in a retrieval system or transmitted in any form or by any means, electronic, photocopying, recording, video recording, or otherwise, without prior permission in writing from the publisher.

ISBN 0 9525509 7 0

Typesetting by STF, Co. Kildare, Ireland.
Printed by ColourBooks Ltd., Baldoyle, Dublin 13, Ireland.

INTRODUCTION

Jiddhu Krishnamurti was born in 1895 in a small town called Madanapalle in South India. He was the eighth of nine children. His mother died when he was ten. In 1909 his father moved with his family to a location near Adyar, the international headquarters of the Theosophical Society. In order to get to a nearby beach Krishnamurti (K) and his younger brother, Nityananda, used to walk across the estate of the Theosophical Society. They were noticed by C W Leadbetter, a leading light in the Society, who was greatly impressed by K's aura. He predicted that K would be used as a vehicle for the Messiah, or World Teacher, whose coming was awaited by the Theosophists. Through the auspices of Dr Annie Besant, the President of the Society, K and his brother, Nityananda, who were inseparable companions, were taken to England to be educated, with particular emphasis on K's training for his designated role.

In 1911 an organisation called The Order of the Star in the East was set up with the objective of preparing the world for the coming of the World Teacher. K was the Head of the Order, with Dr Besant as its Protector. The Order had branches all over the world. K travelled around the world on speaking tours.

At a meeting in Ommen, Holland, in 1929 K sensationally disbanded the Order. He said that he did not want followers. "The moment you follow someone you cease to follow truth." His contention was that truth could not be found through any sect or religion, but only by freeing oneself from all forms of conditioning. "My only concern is to set men absolutely, unconditionally, free."

Throughout the rest of his long life K did not waver from the philosophy he promulgated in 1929. He didn't see himself as belonging to any race, creed or country. He dedicated his life to speaking throughout the world. His teachings influenced millions. His importance as perhaps the most radically pioneering ground breaker in the field of evolving consciousness during the twentieth, or perhaps any other, century cannot be overstated. I'm not sure how he would react to being described as the founding father of the self help movement in the so called New Age. Although it's probably a fair description, I feel that he'd prefer to be remembered as a revolutionary voice in encouraging people to think for themselves.

K established seven schools, which continue in operation, - one in Ojai, California, one in Brockwood Park, Hampshire, England, and five in India. "The highest function of education is to bring about an integrated individual who is capable of dealing with life as a whole."

K died in Ojai on 17 February 1986. He had asked that there should be no funeral ceremonies. His body was cremated and its ashes were distributed between Ojai, England, and India, where they were scattered in the River Ganges..

I had already written an introduction to this book when I remembered that not long after K's death I woke up one morning with a strong impression that he was sitting on the end of my bed. Actually, it was more than an impression; I had a faint visual image of him as through a haze. He seemed to be saying something about writing a book. I put the experience out of my mind, thinking that it was probably some form of hallucination. I'd have felt it utterly presumptuous of me even to imagine that such a well known, awe inspiring, figure as K would wish to undertake such a venture with me. Also, at that time, while I was completely at home with the notion of communication between the spirit and physical worlds, I didn't want to have any public association with an identifiable "dead" historical celebrity.

Since 1978 I had (and have) been in constant daily communication with spirit guides/guardian angels. I have never seen anything unusual about that. It seems to me to be the most natural thing in the world.

During a fifteen year period from 1981 to 1996 I collaborated with a spirit being, known to me as Shebaka, in writing a series of books entitled *The Grand Design*. I published the books in five volumes during the period 1987 to 1996. Earlier this year the five books were edited into two volumes and published by Hampton Roads Publishing Company in Virginia, USA.

The name Shebaka appealed to me because it had no historical associations for me. I didn't find out until 1996 that Shebaka had been a "real" live person who reigned as King of Egypt from 712 to 698 BC. He had been responsible for preserving in stone (now in the British Museum and named after him) what remained of the story of creation according to the god, Ptah; some of the scroll on which it had been recorded had been partially destroyed by worms.

While, as I said above, I had no difficulty with the idea of communication with guardian angels or the world of spirit generally, I don't want to give an impression that writing and publishing *The Grand Design* books happened without a lot of soul searching on my part, including, inevitably I suppose self questionings about my sanity. I remember hearing or reading somewhere that Carl Jung, the eminent psychiatrist, once said – "Show me somebody who is sane and I'll cure him". Whether he said it or not, it sounded like a comforting statement to me, particularly way back when I would sometimes have been inclined to regard myself as an exception in either a sane or an insane world. The changes in consciousness that evolved during the last quarter of the twentieth century and are continuing in the present century have been so astronomical that it's easy to forget how enclosed was earlier societal thinking. It was more civilised than to lead to the burnings at the stake that featured in earlier centuries, but I suspect that it wasn't all that much less judgmental.

In any event, having got over the qualms I had about identifiable public personages, I recorded during 1998 a number of dialogues with Margaret Anna Cusack (1829 – 1899), who was internationally famous as the Nun of Kenmare. I published those dialogues in 1999 in a book entitled *A Free Spirit*. I had barely finished writing that book when K obviously felt I was now ready to work with him – which I feel very privileged to have done.

In line with his 1929 declaration K was at great pains to distance himself from any attempt to set him up as a guru or an authoritative purveyor of "truth", continuing to maintain that each person had to find his/her own truth. Yet even he could hardly have hoped to escape the inevitable dilemma facing the teacher who wants his/her audience to focus on the teachings rather than the teacher. Communicating from a different dimension, a non-physical state of being, may be the most effective way of achieving that aim. As he said in one of our sessions, it makes it easier to be ego-less. It also, perhaps, separates the teachings from being categorised on the basis of perceived merits or shortcomings on the part of the teacher, which tends to be the lot of the human teacher; perceptions that are as variable as the conditioned belief systems of the perceivers.

I don't know what any of K's admirers (I had better not use the word "followers"!) will make of this book if they happen to read it. I take it on trust and I'm presenting it on that basis. I found it a challenging book to write, and, also, a very joyful and hopeful experience.

I dropped my surname in all my previously self-published books and called myself Patrick Francis. In a recent Spanish translation and in the American publications of *The Grand Design* I have used the name I'm generally known by, which is Paddy McMahon. I only mention this to avoid confusion.

August 2001.

ONE
26 October 1998

My role was to ask questions

When I woke this morning I had a very strong impression that J. Krishnamurti wanted to collaborate with me in writing a book. I'm waiting to see whether anything will come through from him.

Yes. Greetings. I'm going to have to experiment with this for awhile until we see how we get on.

Why do you want to do this? Isn't there enough written by you and about you?

A communicator never passes up an opportunity to communicate. Some people may like to hear from me.

Since I came to know about you I have admired you, so I'll be greatly honoured if you wish to use me as a conduit. You'll have to bear with me, though, as I don't feel quite ready to get into another book just yet.

I just wanted to introduce myself to get you attuned to the idea. You can play around with your clocks – I have no need of them.

Why me?

Because you're on my wavelength and you'll understand what

I'm hoping to say.

> I don't feel like doing much today. Is there anything in particular you'd like to say before I "shut down"?

Many of my listeners and readers were often frustrated with me because I didn't pigeonhole my ideas. My role, as I saw it, was to ask questions, not to provide answers. The questions were provocative and were intended to shake the foundations of conditioning, to help people free themselves from thought traps, so that they could find their own way rather than follow a route prescribed for them by somebody else.

> Truth is a pathless land, you said.

Yes, but is it a land at all, even a pathless one?

TWO
17 December

I'm joyful

Thank you for resuming contact with me. I don't want to put pressure on you, but I would prefer not to have to sit around, metaphorically speaking, until you're ready to receive me. I never liked waiting and I haven't changed. I was a fast driver, you know!

> That rings a bell. I read it somewhere. But you're not constrained by time schedules, are you? You have no need of clocks, you said.

No, but you are. I want to be sure that I can make my broadcast, so to speak.

> That sounds a bit ominous. Are you suggesting that I'm likely to be joining you in the spirit dimension soon?

No, I'm not. But there are going to be many demands on your time next year and I might have to take a back seat – which never suited me!

> I have often wished I could ask you how you felt when you left your body. From your books or what I have read about you it wasn't clear to me whether you believed in soul continuity or not.

Yes, of course I believed in it. I just didn't want to be a washboard.

What do you mean by washboard?

People washed their clothes by rubbing them on washboards. The washboard was a cleansing mechanism. What good would it do people if, by rubbing off me, as it were, they considered themselves to be cleansed, i.e., saved? I could have set up another religion, or it could have been set up around my teachings –that's if people knew what to make of them.

What was your legacy then – confusion?

For some, yes. Confusion can be a healthy thing if it's a prelude to questioning, to finding one's own way.

Do you feel you were right not to agree to be a guru?

Wouldn't I be rightly shanghaied now if people had started praying to me!

Anyway, how did you feel?

There were no surprises. I felt great, if you must know. I wasn't confronted by any avenging deity sending me to outer darkness or eternal hellfire because of my irreverence. I continued where I left off, really.

You mean discussing, exploring?

Yes.There were lots of interested fellow travellers waiting for me. While I had cared for my body and it had served me well for a long time, it couldn't withstand the ravages of age indefinitely. It was good to be free of it as a tired old vehicle and replace it with a young, lighter, model.

Are you happy?

I'm joyful.

Is that different from being happy?

I'm not being semantic. To me there's a difference. Joy doesn't have any trimmings or expectations. It's a present feeling. The word "happy" seems to impose conditions. "I'm happy as long as my present state continues" – but will it? When I say I'm joyful – full of joy – there are no strings attached. That's how I am, now and always.

Maybe I can say you're happily joyful?

If you like. Joy seems to cover everything as far as I'm concerned.

Are you a holy one, a saint?

Would you crucify me? I'm wholly joyful!

THREE
18 December
Being aware of now-ness

Many people on earth are under a complete misapprehension in so far as life in spirit is concerned in that they expect it to be totally different from life on earth. It is in some respects, obviously. We don't shoot and kill, or drop bombs on, each other. We're free from the disabilities of physical existence. But mentally we're essentially no different, except in cases where physical defects – like brain damage – had retarded mental capacity, which is restored when the body has fulfilled its mission. We're more aware of the now-ness of life because we're outside of time.

> Would you say that you're happier – sorry, more joyful – now than you were when you were on earth?

Yes, because I'm existing in the now. Being joyful in the now I'm in an ever present state of joy. I'd have wished to have maintained a constant state of joyfulness on earth, but I didn't. Maybe for about two thirds of the time I did.

> If you had that physical life over again what would you have done differently?

In my public life, not much. I had many ups and downs in my private life. I didn't marry the two as well as I might have done.

I was probably too careful of my public image. However, if you don't mind, I don't want to get into dissertations about myself, what I did or didn't do. That seems to me to be totally irrelevant.

> It's just that people would be interested. Maybe you'll relent later on in our dialogue.

Maybe.

> If we're to continue with this project we'll have to find a way for you to come through to me more easily. I'm finding it difficult to receive you just now.

You're not disciplined enough. Early morning is the best time for you but you're not availing yourself of it.

> True. But I haven't heard anything yet that would motivate me to work to a regular time schedule with you. I'm a bit too preoccupied with other things at present to give you the attention you deserve.

I'll hold on.

FOUR
22 December
Creation; how does it happen?

On earth I talked a lot about going beyond thought. That seems to be in conflict with something you've been reading, which purports to come from the highest authority, to the effect that all creation stems from thought. Where does feeling come into the equation? And imagination? Is imagination thought?

Let's consider these questions and see can we arrive at a point of clarity.

Suppose you're taking a walk and you pass by a tree. You stop and look at the tree. Are you feeling, or are you thinking, or are you imagining, or are you doing all three? The tree produces a feeling in you, doesn't it? Then you start to think about that, maybe to consider what is it about the tree that causes the feeling, what sort of a tree is it, etc. What if you were to paint a picture of the tree, how would it look? Now you've moved into the sphere of imagination.

You're inspired by the tree, you resolve to go ahead and paint it and, in due course, you complete your work of art.

What was the starting point in your act of creation? It was the feeling that the tree caused in you, wasn't it? Your thought sought to understand and define the feeling. Your imagination took a leap in the dark, bringing on board the idea of a painting and how you'd go about it.

We have a triangle of feeling, thought and imagination, which for the purpose of our exercise, are separate processes. Thought could have sabotaged the whole idea and rendered it stillborn. Questions such as – "How could I do justice to that tree? Where will I get the time? People will laugh at my effort, won't they?" – could have poured into your head. But the feeling prevailed, supported by the imagination, and pushed thought into expanding its horizons.

Thought leads from the known to the known. You may ask – what else can it do? It has to fit whatever it explores into the realm of its understanding. It can only understand what it knows. So I submit that creation would be at a standstill if it were relying primarily on thought.

In my transition from one dimension to another I haven't changed my mind about the need to go beyond thought in order to grow in awareness. Once a way is established of letting feelings have a free rein without caging them within conditioned thought patterns, thoughts will begin to enjoy themselves and gradually allow themselves to take risks.

So then we have arrived at creation stemming from feeling expanding thought aided by imagination leading to action.

FIVE
24 December
I was expected to be a guru

I'd like to talk about gurus. I was expected to be a guru and I tried to avoid being labelled like that. For most of my public life, that is, once I decided to release myself from the role which had been decreed for me by others, I repeatedly gave my view that people needed to get away from giving their power to those who claim to know the way to truth.

> But if people didn't share their beliefs, etc., wouldn't there be stagnation? Aren't we inspired by the example of others?

As you know, there's a world of difference between sharing one's truth and declaring it to be the way, or the only way.

> Isn't that what Jesus is reported to have done? "I am the way, the truth and the life", or words to that effect. Isn't that what others have done, and do?

I don't want to get into personalities. The life and words of Jesus were recorded selectively. Ask yourself, though – if it is so that Jesus encouraged people to be as he was, how many of his so called followers have ever done so, or would have regarded themselves as his equals? Of what use is it to humans crying out for compassion and hope to regard Jesus as a God who will one day sit in judgment on them and consign them to eternal heaven or eternal hell? Is there anybody at all on your planet – I mean anybody who would declare himself/herself to be a follower of Jesus or Buddha or any of the other religious leaders – who would say to the world, or even to himself/herself – "I am as good as Jesus or Buddha or any of those who have been singled out as higher beings"?

> I doubt it. They would probably regard it as blasphemy or something like that.

What does that tell you? Surely that so called gurus, whether they are self styled or put into that category against their will, perhaps posthumously, haven't helped humans much in the area of self esteem. I'm making no judgments about personalities, only about the effects of movements or organizations that subsequently grew, or grow , up around them. That's what happens with gurus – which may not be their intention at all. In any event, the effects on awareness have always been more negative than positive.

> We always need help. Where would we be without the interchange of ideas, the sharing of experience?

I'm not talking about that. As I have said, sharing is an altogether different thing from imposing or presenting from a position of dogmatic authoritarianism.

> But surely people need answers. If those who know won't inform those who don't know, how can we ever progress in awareness?

Each person's journey is different. If I may presume to say so, what one needs is to follow one's own truth, not anybody else's.

> That could be a lonely journey then.

Not at all. Trying to follow somebody else's lead is a sure way to loneliness. If all people were to follow their own individual truths with respect for each others' truths your planet would be a haven of joy.

In so far as those who know not telling those who don't know is concerned, essentially and ultimately all anybody has the capacity to share, or indeed know, is his or her own truth. If you share your truth with others, that may help them, or some of them, to find theirs. But it won't be yours. It may correspond with yours in many ways, but no two people's truths are exactly the same. And that's the beauty of life. Would you have it any other way?

>   No. So I can take it that "gurudom" doesn't find favour with you?!

I wonder whatever could have given you that idea!

SIX
29 December

My truth is I am

May I ask you what's your truth? And is it different now from what it was when you were on earth?

My truth is I am.

Is that it? Is that all you're going to say about it? What more do you want me to say? That statement is fully comprehensive. I know that I am. Have you a better way of expressing your truth?

No, I don't suppose so. What about my second question?

My truth isn't any different now from what it was when I was on earth. Perhaps I feel more affirmed in it.

But there's a bigger – or, at least, another – question. What about you in relation to all other souls and a Source/Creator/God?

I know that I exist. I am. All else seems to me to be a continuing exploration. I took on the form of Jiddhu Krishnamurti for a number of earth years and now I have moved on to another dimension. When I say I **am** there are no limits. I am as I am in each continuing expression of me. I'm not anybody else, so I cannot express anybody else's truth. I understand that I share the universe with others and I'm delighted to be able to discuss and explore with as many of them as wish to do so.

Are you asking me how did I come to be, and how do I know I'm going to continue to be?

> That's contained in my question, I think.

I don't know how I came to be. I know I am. I'm certainly not going to continue to be as I am because I'm evolving from moment to moment, so to speak. I am as I am in continual motion. By motion I don't mean movement.

> I believe that we're all part of God or a Source, that that's how we have life, that that's how we are; that it's that divinity in us that binds us all together and yet gives each of us uniquely individual, eternal expression. How does that fit in with your truth?

You don't like to think that you might be a haphazard happening, do you? Why does there have to be a Source – or a God, if you prefer? You're still caught in a seeming logic that nothing can exist without some agency or power causing it to exist. Wouldn't it be disturbing to think that there's nobody pulling the strings at all?

> But there's something that drives us, isn't there? If we don't call it God then maybe love would be more acceptable?

Let me relate your question to my truth. Yes, I accept that I'm truly expressing myself when I love unreservedly, unconditionally. That may well be true for all others. They would have to answer for themselves. If you want to call that the divine in me I have no objection.

> But you don't believe in a Source, as such?

I neither believe nor disbelieve. All I know is I am.

SEVEN
30 December

Love is the regulatory energy of the universe

I don't want to give an impression that I'm an isolationist. I believe totally in the interconnectedness of all life and that what I am and how I am affects all others. Obviously, it follows that the more an unconditionally loving vibration goes out from me, the more harmonious the universe is. If that's so for me I accept that it's likely to be so for all others. Thus I can say with reasonable certainty that love is the regulatory energy of the universe in how it's expressed – that is, to the extent that it's conditional or unconditional.

If you want to say that unconditional love is God, or vice versa, that's fine by me. The thing is, though, not to get confused by word play. The word "God" has such emotive and misleading connotations through its religious usage that I prefer to bypass it. I can tell you for sure that the God of your religions is non-existent – a monstrosity born out of fear and/or lust for power and control.

EIGHT
1 January 1999

Nothing doing

This book is being written in a sporadic sort of way. I haven't really settled into it yet. If it's to be done I want to do it justice and to give Krishnaji the respect and attention he deserves.

Anyway, on this the first morning of a new year I'm waiting to see if he wants to communicate.

Later. Nothing doing this morning. He doesn't seem to be on the line, or else he feels I'm not clear headed enough to receive him. Either way, I'm calling it a day.

NINE
2 January
No more double think

I wonder could you give me a signal whenever you're ready to communicate so that I won't have to sit around waiting?

I have no difficulty about communicating at any time. The trouble is that I have to go through one of your watchdogs to make an appointment.

You mean my guides?

That's what you like to call them! They're very efficient, I can tell you. You're well minded.

That's because I asked them not to let anybody through except by arrangement; they know when it's okay. I have exercised my free will in that way. I thank them. Thank you, too, for letting me know the position where you are concerned.

There are many people attempting to raise consciousness at present. They're doomed to failure if they continue to work from illusory foundations.

How do you mean?

Total clarity is needed. For a start, there's too much double think around the notion of God. People can't have it both ways. They seem to subscribe – or, at least, some do – to the idea of a supreme being, but yet that that being is in each soul. You have some so called avatars even claiming to be that supreme being and demanding devotion from mindless followers who have surrendered their powers of discrimination. People are being asked to accept the dichotomy of there being an entity called God, or whatever, who is both separate from them and in them. At the same time they're being asked to accept that there's no separation, that we're all one. How can people come to terms with such contortionism?

> I suppose we find it hard to accept that we're totally in charge of our own destiny. We feel more secure if we believe that there's somebody out there in control – piloting the plane, as it were. So we tend to look for one or more who we hope will fulfil that function for us.

And, of course, there's always somebody ready to fill that slot and exercise the power that goes with it.

> It's asking a lot of us to let go of all supports. Speaking for myself, I don't feel strong enough or wise enough or capable enough. For example, I feel that I can't, nor do I want to, do without the help of my guides.

I'm not suggesting that you do. That's a different thing altogether. The key question is – do you feel equal to your guides?

> Yes, unquestionably. My understanding is that we have a cooperative arrangement, freely entered into on both sides before I was born into this incarnation, and that I'm availing myself of their expertise in the same way as I would, for instance, that of a plumber or electrician – or yours, for that matter.

And you have no doubt that you're my equal?

None whatever. That doesn't mean that I regard myself as having your mental capacity or knowledge, wisdom, etc. You're you and I'm me, if I may put it like that.

In our search for clarity let me be clear. There's no confusion about looking for all the help you feel you need from those whom you consider to be in a position to help you, provided you understand and accept that they're not superior beings to you, that, in fact, there's no being in the whole universal scheme of things who is superior to you. Now there's no separation, don't you see? You still have as much support as you want. And there's no more double think.

TEN

7 January

Reincarnation is an opportunity for growth in awareness

May I ask you about reincarnation? What are your views on it?

It's an aspect of life. Souls indulge in it.

Is it helpful?

That depends on the soul reincarnating. It's an opportunity for growth in awareness, let's put it like that.

Your arrival was heralded by all sorts of predictions. You were to be the new Messiah, the World Teacher, the vessel for the Master Maitreya, etc. While in your early life you paid homage to the Masters, as they were called, you later let go of all that. Were you a victim of delusion in the early part of your life – or perhaps later?

Neither. It was all part of a process I needed to undergo. Opening people's minds to freedom and its implications was my objective. I had to be free in myself before I could tease out with others what freedom meant to me.

Did that mean that you no longer believed in the Masters, or you sidelined them, or what?

It wasn't – or isn't – a question of belief. It meant that I had come to the conclusion that nobody but myself could manifest my truth for me.

Wasn't that what the Masters would be helping you to do?

Things get confused when some are seen as the embodiment of truth, or that one cannot arrive at one's truth without going through them. What freedom is there in that way?

Could your approach be seen as arrogant?

Perhaps. But of what concern is that to me? Actually, it's not arrogant. It's realistic. I'm not casting a reflection on anybody or setting myself above anybody. But neither am I prostrating myself before anybody nor in any way negating or denigrating my own uniqueness. All I'm saying is that I am – as I've already said, if you remember. That's not taking away from, or dishonouring, anybody else.

Do you propose to reincarnate?

No. I lived long enough on my last sojourn!

ELEVEN

9 January

Your reality is yourself, what you create from within

I have been re-reading what I have already written. I still find it hard to believe that K is actually communicating with me. How did I ever get into this sort of thing? Yet I want to continue with it. If it's real it must be worthwhile. That's the question. Is it real? I have to believe it is. Like K says – I am. So I must continue to be as I am.

There's a character in Star Trek – Deep Space Nine – called Oto. To look at, he seems real, physically substantial. Then at times he disappears and reappears somewhere else in a jelly-like or fluid manifestation out of which the solid physical being re-emerges.

What's the real Oto? I could, perhaps, see him as an example of how we operate. We take on a physical form, a seemingly solid structure, we drop it, we go into a fluid spirit state and we re-appear in another solid structure (a body); not the same body, as in Oto's case, but maybe it's a fair analogy.

I find it sort of mind-boggling when I delve into the conundrum of reality versus illusion.

K may have something to say on the subject.

As you know, your physical body isn't solid at all, although it appears so, and it leaves no doubt about its apparent solidity when it hits against another solid structure; yet, the body is mostly water – fluid. If you knew the technique, you could manipulate your body – like Oto.

> Can you teach me that technique?

What would be the point? How would that help you?

> For example, I could get from one place to another without having to use transport. If all people, or even some, could use it, there wouldn't be any traffic jams, no sitting for hours in cars, no queuing for buses, no waiting around at airports.

And what about all the people who'd be out of employment?

In any event, we have moved into irrelevancy. At the present stage of human evolution the restrictiveness of the solid structures helps to create a point of focus. How to find freedom within the restriction is the challenge. People often need to be put up against the wall, so to speak, before they pay attention.

Your reality is yourself, what you create from within. You know that. What's mind-boggling about it? Whomever or whatever you see or are in contact with have their reality for you in your perception of them. That doesn't mean that they are illusions. They have their own reality for themselves. You in your reality are constant, although evolving, in your relationship with yourself. But, as others view you, you're likely to have a different reality in so far as each of them is concerned. There are all sorts of different yous, although there may be many points of agreement in others' perception of you.

When I talk about being forced to pay attention, then, what I mean is that you as you are in your human manifestation are presented with the spiritual truth of yourself as the creation of all that you are – that is, through your feelings, your thoughts, your imagination, as we discussed earlier. The illusion is in the non-understanding of that, and, through that non-understanding, continually seeking to impose an externalised caricature on yourself.

TWELVE
19 February
Why would I want to be confined by answers?

In your re-reading of Pupul's book (*J. Krishnamurti: A Biography*) you have been thinking that I went through all sorts of mental gyrations about mind and brain and thoughts and observer and observed, and so on. Well, you needn't feel awkward about that. You're right. I agree with you. I was making myself so obscure that hardly anybody could follow me – I mean follow my line of exploration. I became concerned about the preservation of my teachings; but who was going to be able to explain them?

> You maintained that it was your teachings, not you yourself, that were important. It would seem to me, though, that you and your approach embodied your teachings – in other words, how you questioned rather than answered. In your case, I wonder is it presumptuous of me to regard the word "teachings" as a misnomer. "Teachings " as a word implies answers, I think. "Questionings" might be more appropriate where you are concerned. You stressed the importance of asking questions that have no answers.

Yes, and I still do.

> What would be an example of such a question?

How did life/God/love come to be? You have been told that it has always been. How can that be explained?

If I was born, I lived for X number of years and I died, there's no challenge to your understanding. But here I am, alive and well. Some people might say to me, in accordance with their beliefs, that ultimately I'll merge – or re-merge – with God. Others might say that I'll continue to evolve, indefinitely expressing myself in whatever form I choose. Still others might say that I'm going to have to submit to some Divine Judgment and be consigned to eternal Heaven or Hell. These are all just musings, with a smattering of convenient dogma. They are not answers. And I haven't even touched on the original question I asked.

> Does it bother you that, in your view, such a question can't be answered?

Not in the least. Why should it? That's what makes life so interesting, journeying into the unknown. Why would I want to be confined by answers?

> Then, may I go back to my speculation that the word "teachings" contains an implication of answers? Or does it?

Why should it?

THIRTEEN
27 March

Ah! Expectation!

It's over a month since I had my last dialogue with K. I have been caught up with other things and I didn't have the energy, or indeed the inclination, to get on with this. So I don't know what sort of a reaction I'm going to get – if any. I have to admit that I don't feel the same sense of ease of relationship with K that I have with Shebaka or Margaret.

If you understood anything of what I presented, you must know that I wasn't into making judgments. I'm hardly likely to have changed. I think you're perceiving me, sensing me, as more detached than your other communicators. That's my way of not intruding on your space, so that you can be neutral about me, if you wish.

You were somewhat disturbed by seeming contradictions between my teachings and my behaviour according to Radha (*Lives in the Shadow with J. Krishnamurti* by Radha Rajagopal Sloss). I'm not asking you to be my advocate. As I said earlier, all that's irrelevant. It's easy to make judgments about people – but who's in a position to do so truly? I don't seek to deny that I had human failings as Jiddhu Krishnamurti. Why should I? I lived that life in a search for my truth, and my aim was to help others in their search. Any soul who chooses to incarnate physically with the object of helping to raise awareness consciously runs the risk of being branded as a hypocrite or worse if his/her behaviour doesn't fit into a perceived pattern of conformist social or religious norms. Surely an added value of such a life is that it challenges all conditioning in its physical expression as well as in whatever it presents as its vision of truth?

Yes. Thanks. What would you like to discuss today?

I'll tell you a little story. Two men, life long friends, who had reached what I might call the late autumn or early winter of their lives, were relaxing during one of their regular outings together. I'll call them A and B to avoid any nationalistic overtones. Aided by somewhat generous liquid refreshment, they became unusually introspective. They talked about their early lives, their dreams, their hopes, their careers, their romances, and how some things worked out well and others didn't. Inevitably maybe, the conversation switched from the past to the future. They agreed that, in the natural order of things, they didn't have much time left to live. What then? They were religious in a conformist sort of way, but, when it came down to brass tacks, they weren't sure whether they believed in an afterlife or not. They certainly had no concept of what it might be like. So they made a pact that whoever of them died first would come back to tell the other what to expect – provided that there was any continuation. They accepted that if the first to go didn't make any contact that wouldn't necessarily constitute empirical evidence that there was an afterlife, since there might be no means of communication. However, they'd do their damnedest, in a manner of speaking.

Some years passed. Occasionally they reminded each other of their pact. A suffered a severe, but mercifully brief, illness. Before he died he spoke to B about their pact and promised that he'd do his best to honour it.

Days, weeks and months went by and B hadn't heard anything from his friend – or certainly wasn't aware of any communication from him. He decided that when people died they died, and that was that. He felt a mixture of disappointment and relief, but perhaps more strongly than either, sadness that he wouldn't ever see his friend again.

Then, one night when he was sitting by himself half-asleep in his sitting room, he got a strong feeling that A was in the room with him. Fully awake now, he looked around but couldn't see anything. He said to himself that his imagination was playing tricks on him. Then, clear as a bell, he heard a voice in his ear - "No, it's not". Next he caught a glimpse of A, large as life, then another and another. He rubbed his eyes, wondering was he "seeing things", but the impressions and images didn't go away. He was surprised to find that he was a bit frightened in spite of his delight that maybe it was his friend honouring their pact.

Let's reconstruct their dialogue.

    A What are you afraid of? Didn't I promise to come back?

    B I know. But I'm not sure it's really you.

    A Who else could it be?

    B It could be me going mad. Or somebody pretending to be you.

    A Like who?

    B The devil. Weren't we told that he does that sort of thing?

    A My mother used to call me a little devil, right enough.

    B It's really you, is it?

    A Yes, it's really me. So you needn't be in any doubt that there's an afterlife.

B What's it like?

A Great. I can't believe my luck. I have everything I want. Except one thing.

B What's that?

A I miss our meetings and our chats.

B So do I.

A Does that mean that you'd like to join me?

B (hesitantly) Y-yes…..But not yet.

A Why not? Haven't I told you how great it is? Better than anything you could ever imagine.

B I'm not ready to go yet … Tell me, did you meet St Peter?

A Indeed I did. He gave me a great welcome. I mentioned you to him.

B Oh …

A He said your number was coming up.

B What does that mean?

A You can ask him yourself when you see him. I've got to fly.

Is that all?

Yes. That's my little story. Didn't you like it?

I was expecting something more.

Ah! Expectation!

What's the point of the story?

What do you think?

> Fear. We want to know and we're afraid of what we might find. We don't want to let go of what we're used to, however it may be.

Well, then, it has a point, hasn't it?

> Yes. I suppose I was hoping it might be a funny story.

Maybe the joke's on you.

> Fair enough. Why did you bring St Peter into it?

Because of how he's seen – the keeper of the keys to heaven. I used to like stories that included him.

FOURTEEN
1 July

The way to enlightenment

After a lapse of over three months I'm sitting wondering whether K has got fed up waiting for me to be ready to continue with our dialogue.

I understand how difficult it is for you. I want our communication to be as enjoyable as possible – at your pace.

It's just that when I'm feeling tired or mentally sluggish I become doubtful as to whether I can receive you accurately.

Let's see how we get on. On reflection, did you see anything else in the little story I told you?

It's interesting that A (in spirit) said that he missed his meetings and chats with B. Here on earth we find it easy to understand missing somebody who has passed on, but we tend not to think of it being a two way process.

Anything else?

A didn't seem to be much different from the way he was on earth. A common human misconception is that we're transformed into truly enlightened beings when we move on.

The struggle continues. But, of course, there wouldn't be so much of a struggle if people didn't live their lives within such illusory frameworks. I say to anybody who's prepared to listen: free your thinking from all ideologies, theologies, absolutes, all the notions of right and wrong that may have been drummed into you, thereby giving yourself uncluttered opportunities to respond to each moment as it comes, That's the way to enlightenment, to be who you truly are.

My little story was partly a practical joke. That's not to take from the validity of the points you make. You wanted something to lighten up our dialogue, but what you got disappointed you initially. Still, we've had a little less serious interaction, and maybe now you can feel more at home with me. How's that?

Fine. Thanks.

FIFTEEN

7 July

If we can reduce even one mountain to a molehill ...

What do you regard as your purpose in life?

> I didn't expect that question. I suppose – to be – to accept the challenge of freedom – to love unconditionally – and to go with the flow of what follows from all that, which I assume automatically includes expressing myself as creatively as is possible for me. That's the best I can come up with off the top of my head.

Does all that include dialoguing with me in my disembodied state?

> I have no doubt it does. It's the next best thing to doing it with you physically, which I would love to have done if circumstances, including knowing earlier in my life about your existence, had enabled me to do so. But maybe I'm having the best of both worlds now.

You didn't include in your statement of purpose that you're a pioneering agent in bridging the gap between the physical and spirit states. It's a disabling thing for people to move from your planet and never to be heard from again. Why should that be so? Some of your religions have conditioned people to believe that there should be no contact with the "dead". Out of sight, out of mind, sort of thing. So we on this side have to go through all sorts of manoeuvres to get somebody to listen to us.

In your physical body you can't help being aware of the restrictions of time. You know your body's life span is limited and you want to crowd as much as you can into the time you've got left. That's unnecessary pressure. Once there are no limitations there's no pressure.

I lived for my talks. I loved talking to people – and listening to them. I have plenty of opportunities to do that here. But I want to expand my horizons. That's what I've always endeavoured to do. Why should there be any barriers to communication? What are we talking about? Form, isn't it? Once we're no longer controlled by form we can do anything. When I'm communicating with you we're dispensing with form. We're breaking down the barriers of time and space. I'm no longer confined within the image of a twentieth century philosopher. You move out of the restrictions of your ageing body – ageing since you were born.

If the time had been right I could have been more open to the potential of all that when I was on earth. I would have saved myself – and, no doubt, my listeners – the bother of going round and round in abstractions. However, I don't want to minimise my contribution to growth in awareness; it was considerable. (I have gone past the stage of false modesty!)

Now that I'm back in a timeless, unrestricted, zone I'm more aware of the mountains of ignorance that have prevented souls from reaching out to each other beyond the boundaries of time and space. If we can reduce even one mountain to a molehill by what we're attempting we'll have achieved something worthwhile.

SIXTEEN
9 July
Free will is how I express myself divinely

> What more is there to say? Everything is summarised in I am. Words only cause complications and complexities. How much further can we go with this book?

Yes, there comes a point when it's desirable – necessary, even, - to move beyond thought and, consequently, words. But words are the commerce of your daily life, except for somebody who takes a vow of silence and retires to a monastery, or such like. As it happens, I'm not using words to communicate with you, but, in order to record what I seem to be conveying to you, you are interpreting me into words. We can't write a book without words, can we?

> Do you use words in your communication with others in spirit?

I don't need to, but I do because I like doing so. An interesting thing happens, though. Suppose I'm having a discussion with a group. I use certain words which to me seem to represent what I intend to convey. Somebody in the audience questions my use of a particular word or phrase, saying something like – "That doesn't represent accurately what you intended to convey". You see? The risk of misunderstanding is eliminated because of the telepathic link between the audience and myself. In your human state words are taken literally to mean whatever meanings are given to them by your dictionaries or in common parlance, whereas they often only partially, or not at all, convey what the speaker intended. Thus confusion reigns.

> So I run the risk of misinterpreting you when I use words to attempt to articulate what you're transmitting to me.

Yes, you do. And, of course, I'm relying on you to be on my wavelength; so there's risk for me, too. For those who are engaged in bringing about change there has to be risk. Free will is a huge source of risk, isn't it?

> My understanding of free will is that it's a basic, constant ingredient in our being part of God/love. It's therefore total – that is, one hundred per cent unrestricted – and eternal. I don't think you subscribe to all that, do you?

What makes you say that?

> In an earlier session you pooh-poohed the notion of God, or a Source.

I didn't pooh-pooh it. I questioned your need to believe in it, which is a different thing. I said that all I know is I am. I certainly know that as I am I have free will, which nobody questions or seeks to control. I assume that in my continuing existence there will be no change in that position. If you want to say that I'm divine and that free will is how I express myself divinely, that's fine and there's no disagreement between us. Or do you want me to say more on the subject?

> N-no.

A bit doubtful! I have to be honest. I can only speak from what I know. As I keep saying, my only certainty is that I am.

> Agnosticism is perceived, I think, as only applying to the human state.

Human agnosticism would be seen as relating to the continuity of life, which would logically cover such things as belief in God. Obviously, I know that life continues after physical death. So my agnosticism, if you want to call it that, is much broader in its scope than its human relative. I bet that until now you have never encountered a spirit agnostic!

Come to think of it, I have, although not in quite the same way; more in the sense of the ultimate question as to how God (and all souls, in God) has/had no beginning, to which no answer is known, I'm told.

So we're back to I AM, which is the only answer you need.

SEVENTEEN
10 July

Success?

May I tell you another story? Saul was a man of the world, a good businessman, hail fellow well met, married suitably, three children, two male, one female. A man much respected in his community. When he was approaching fifty years of age he was invited to run for Mayor of his city, which he did, successfully. He used his business acumen in the interests of the city, and its inhabitants prospered. Saul's reputation soared. He entered national politics and, in due course, he became the prime minister of his country.

He had reached the pinnacle of public achievement nationally and interacted on equal terms with leaders of other nation states.

With the overwhelming approval of his fellow citizens, Saul continued in public office as prime minister until he reached the age of sixty-six, when he decided that the time had come for him to retire. Showered with accolades and tributes from all sides he retreated into relative obscurity, with occasional reminders of his existence in the national media.

After a brief illness, Saul died at the age of ninety. Tributes poured in, nationally and internationally. Thousands of words were written in respectful obituaries. His place in the history of the nation was assured.

Religion had not featured prominently in Saul's life, although he didn't question the beliefs to which he had been conditioned as a child. Politically, it was advantageous for him to project a safe, conformist image.

After he left his body, Saul was, of course, presented with immediate proof of his continuing existence. He was an interested observer at all the formalities of his funeral. He was welcomed into his new state by many relatives, friends and former colleagues. He was delighted to be free of his aged body.

So far you have been content to go along with the story, but now I can see that you're somewhat impatient, wondering what's the point of it.

> Ordinarily, I wouldn't care whether there was a point or not, but I feel that it wouldn't merit inclusion in our book unless it had some impact for the reader.

Please bear with me. I'm not trying to be smart, really.

From a human standpoint, Saul's life on earth was hugely successful. He was widely respected, both nationally and internationally. His actions affected the lives of many people – for the most part, positively, at least materially. He had the wisdom to retire while he was still at the top, with the majority of his colleagues and the population generally wanting him to stay.

A relevant question is – how well did his life on earth serve him as a platform for his transition into his non-physical state? His perceived success as businessman and politician, as well as husband and father, is of no use as a barometer, since it's an external indication only. Ultimately, the answer lies in his internal – spiritual, if you like, -response to all his experiences, relationships, and so on. The only indicator of his response in my story, as I told it, is in his unquestioning acceptance of his religious conditioning. On that basis, in spite of all his achievements and renown, he was ill-prepared for his transition. In saying that, I don't mean to imply that it was a mistake for him to get involved in business and political life. In any case, he had lots of time after his retirement to look inwards.

> Yet he was happy to have left his body and he was welcomed by friends and relatives. So wasn't that fine?

Yes, of course. Nobody is excluded from a welcoming transition except those who don't want it, usually because they don't want to accept that they have left the earth plane.

In telling the story of Saul I wanted to illustrate how misleading may be yardsticks of success and failure, as commonly perceived in human terms. In so far as growth in his spiritual awareness is concerned, I submit that, on the basis of the evidence provided in the story, Saul might as well not have been born at all.

> But yet he experienced life on a physical plane. He was, apparently, content in his personal life, and he had all the excitement and fulfilment of successful careers in business and politics, as well as earning the respect and admiration of his fellow citizens. He was happy to die when he did, and he seemed to adjust well to his new state. Surely all that was worthwhile? Didn't he express his spirituality through the way he was in himself and through all his activities?

What you're saying is valid on one level – that of passing experience. But who was doing the experiencing? Was it Saul or was it the image of himself that he had created? My proposition is that it was the latter – the image.

> But he left all that behind when he retired from public life. If he was so involved with his image, surely he wouldn't have turned aside voluntarily from all the status and para-

phernalia of power that would have automatically served to bolster his image? It was as if he said – "I've had it all. I don't need it anymore. It's time to let somebody else take over and for me to do something different – or nothing – away from the glare of publicity during my remaining years".

Suppose he retired in order to preserve his public image at its zenith, and, indeed, to enhance it, by his apparent selfless patriotism in handing over power to somebody younger? Might not the effect of his life then have been the creation of a monument to his ego and his place in history?

EIGHTEEN
11 July

We're endlessly creative

I've been thinking about your Saul story. I see the point of your questions. But, given the thrust of what you're saying – all you know is "I am" – what difference does it make whether he was living through his image or not? After he left his body he was welcomed into his new state by many friends and, presumably, continued to live happily. Why would he bother with probing into the mysterious, and perhaps confusing, depths of philosophical questionings that he might well feel have no relevance for him?

What I'm getting at is this: many people find great security in belief in a God who arranges everything, including their final destiny. Their goal is to find eternal happiness with their God in Heaven. It doesn't matter that they may not have any clear concept of what life would be like in Heaven.

Even though when they pass on they don't come face to face with God, since they don't have any clear concept of Heaven they can accept that that's where they are, with immediate fulfilment of all their wishes and no restrictions. Why look for anything more?

Because we're endlessly creative. Life is never stagnant. I can't be a zombie and I assume that neither can anybody else. On earth people have to strive for things – jobs, money, etc., - and a lot of their energy goes into that struggle, with all its attendant worries. In the spirit state there's no need for jobs or money; whatever one needs is immediately available by imagining it. And there's no need for sleep either. So all the conundrums that take up so much time on earth have no relevance in spirit. Even time itself, which is such a central preoccupation on earth, doesn't feature at all in spirit.

Imagine yourself in that situation, with everything you ever wanted immediately to hand at the press of a button, so to speak, and never having to bother about being tired or hungry or ill, what would you do with yourself? Would you be content to continue indefinitely in an unquestioning acceptance of your state of being as you now find it?

May I suggest that you consider those questions and we'll resume our dialogue when you feel like doing so.

NINETEEN

12 July

The unknown can never be known or it is no longer the unknown

I'd certainly enjoy without reservation having the luxury to be the way you've posited.

I think that the most honest way I can arrive at an answer to your question is to look at what has driven me to write the books I've already written and what's impelling me to work on this book.

An obvious motivation is money. I can dismiss that, since my initial intention back in the early eighties was to write whatever was coming to me and leave the material there to be discovered or not after I had moved on. Later, after I had begun to publish the books, I avoided any suggestion of aggressive marketing. I think I can honestly say that I'm not concerned about whether the books make a lot of money or not. I'd like them to be available, though, to people who may be interested in reading them – which, I suppose, means that money comes into the equation to some extent, at least.

Am I looking for notoriety? The same considerations hold true, I think. At the same time, I have to admit that, while

I'm reclusive and I like being anonymous, I also like to be well known. That's a self-contradictory statement, I know, but it's factual nonetheless. Maybe it's a case of wanting to have things both ways.

In asking the question as you did you have given me scope to be self-indulgent in replying. I hope I'm not being too much so. It seems to me, though, that, if I can answer it truly, my answer will have relevance for others.

Including me.

That would be something! Are you serious?

Yes, deadly (!) so. This is a crunch question and I'll develop it from my point of view later.

When I go into it, being well known or not isn't of much relevance to me in the long run. I'm almost sixty-six years of age and in the natural order of things I wouldn't have much longer to enjoy my fame! In any event, I'm already relatively well known because of my existing books. So I'll let that consideration go.

I need to consider whether I write simply because I like to do so. Why, then, do I choose to write what may be called "channelled" books rather than to have a go at novels or plays or biographies or something on those lines, which was my original intention years ago before I got into the "paranormal" stuff? Strangely, or perhaps not, since I got into this line of writing, trying my hand at, say, novels or plays, even if I could be assured of doing so with acclaimed artistic and literary merit, no longer held, or holds, any appeal for me.

Now I've reached the stage, after self-examination, where I can say that I write this kind of book because I want to more than anything else. Why? Because, through the exploration process involved in the writing, I have reached into myself in a way that has brought me peace, bliss even. I have found a philosophy and a way of being which make complete sense to me. I love the exploration, the challenge of the freedom to *be*, without prejudice, rules, fixed beliefs, rigidity of any kind; in other words, to be totally open to the flow of life. I continue to write because there seems to be no end to that process, nor to the wonder and joy that goes with it.

My answer to your question, then, has to be no. Irrespective of what my external circumstances might be I would still want to have continuing scope to express myself as creatively as I possibly could. I must; it's the way I am.

Now you see why your answer is relevant for me, too. Considered superficially, my teaching might appear to be nihilistic. But, when I say that I AM is my only certainty, I have the whole universe of exploration open to me. I know no limits. If you say to me that God is the unknown, or the unknown is God, then I can say to you that I believe in God with all my being. That concept presents to me a voyage of endless discovery. The unknown can never be known or it is no longer the unknown. So my universe is always evolving, always revealing new aspects of itself to me, as I am to myself. We are one in the unknowingness, which allows me to be eternally creative in my expression of I AM.

Does it follow, then, that I know that I am, but I don't know who or what I am?

Yes, that's the wonder and the beauty of it, don't you see? When I say I am I accept my being totally. When I say I don't know who or what I am I place no boundaries on myself. If that's so for me, it's reasonable for me to accept that it's so for you and for all others. That's why I could say about our friend Saul that he might as well not have been born into that particular physical life if he allowed himself to be fenced in by a rigidly conformist belief system.

Now, if you want me to say that I am God, or you are God, or they are God, that's fine with me, because what I'm saying is that I'm the unknown, or part of the unknown, and so are you, and so are all others. We're all one in our unknowingness and individual in how we are within it. Can you comprehend the freedom of that? Can you feel it? It's miraculous, isn't it?

TWENTY
13 July
An infinity of non-answers, or unknown

> A book of yours that greatly impressed me was *Freedom From The Known*. We're back to that, really, aren't we?

To some extent, yes. What I was talking about, of course, in that book was freedom from conditioning, all the beliefs, etc., which have fenced us in and in many ways made us fearful creatures. In what we're discussing now we have left the known behind because it's of no help to us, or I should say that we, I – I had better not be presumptuous – have encapsulated the known into the simplicity of I AM, and from that base I'm free to explore the unknown without any restrictions.

> May I ask what's your purpose in continuing to explore the unknown? I know that's a repetitive question in view of what has come up in our most recent sessions, but I feel that elaboration would be helpful.

Primarily, my purpose is to express my creativity. If you look at the history of the human species, you'll see that there have been people in every century who have explored ways and means of breaching existing boundaries of perception and methodology. That's particularly obvious in the development of technology, which is moving at such a pace that people would find it impossible to conceptualise what even the next decade may manifest.

It has always been my nature to question and probe. Why would I be any different now?

> If we stay with technology as an example, those who are involved in that area are, of course, expressing their creativity, but they are also very definitely looking for answers. Are you?

Yes and no. All the technological developments, your methods of transport, communication, labour saving devices, are, generally, geared towards making life easier for people. In so far as I'm concerned, though, I'm not included in "people" any longer and I don't need to have life made easier for me. It couldn't be any easier than it is, and I have all the technological answers to hand, if you like, or, more accurately, I have transcended any need for them.

The question you've asked is a difficult one for me to answer. If there is an unknown, as I have postulated, it follows that I don't know the extent of it. I may be able to chip away at it, in a manner of speaking, and arrive at answers that I didn't previously know, and yet may not reduce what's still unknown – if you know what I mean!

The notion of infinity is itself a non-answer. If there could be an answer to it, or an understanding of it, it wouldn't be infinity. I can extrapolate from that that there's an infinity of non-answers, or unknown So anybody who tries to pin down, or box in any way, the unknown – God, if you like - is going down a blind alley. I'm not about to get myself into that bind.

I can say, yes, I'm looking for answers, and, no, I'm not looking for an ultimate answer beyond which there are no further questions. If that point were ever to be reached there would be an end to creativity. I suggest that that cannot be.

TWENTY-ONE
14 July

There's no such thing as being interrupted as far as I'm concerned

I have been relating the concept of the unknown to my own human situation. Even though I realise that how my future will unfold is determined by how I live in the present, there are times when I'd love to be able to see, say, what my situation will be a year from now, or the outcome of a particular project. On the other hand, when I'm starting to read a book I don't want to know in advance how it's going to unfold, or, if I'm interested in, say, a football or a tennis match, I want to be able to enjoy the match without knowing the result. By and large, I'm finding that there's much more enjoyment in life when each day unfolds spontaneously. Then I can savour the wonder of the unexpected. Life would be very dull, I think, if I knew what each day, week, month, year had in store for me. That would make a nonsense of free will, too, wouldn't it? Exercising choice wouldn't enter into the equation at all. I might as well be a robot.

The more I think about it, the more the idea of an eternal unknown appeals to me. Even within the framework of my own human experience I can see what a wonderful thing it is.

At a stage in my life when I was still very much influenced by religious conditioning I used wonder what would there be to do in Heaven. If we were all going to be sitting around, or, more likely, kneeling, adoring God endlessly, I thought, rather guiltily, that that wouldn't be much to look forward to. No matter how I looked at it, the prospect wasn't very stimulating.

By way of contrast, I can begin to comprehend, if only vaguely, the awesome magnificence of ever present possibilities of creative expression/evolving consciousness in the context of timeless existence in a state of total bliss.

I'm resuming the dialogue with K, I hope, if he's free.

I'm always free.

Suppose you're in the middle of a discussion with a group, or an individual, you may not like to be interrupted.

It's hard for you to understand, but there's no such thing as being interrupted as far as I'm concerned. I can give you my attention and also, simultaneously, communicate with others. I'm no longer in a linear progression of happenings or consciousness.

How do you know when I'm ready to work with you?

Thoughts project themselves in waves. I don't have to check in with your minders any more, since you have, as it were, cleared the lines. In any case, I wait for you to contact me whenever is convenient for you. When you send out a thought that you're ready to link up with me, that thought flashes through to me like a ray of light.

If I send a thought to any soul in spirit, does it work like that?

Yes, it does, unless, of course, they shut themselves off, which they can do, if they so wish. They're entitled to their privacy, too!

> So, while we're cooperating on this book, when I send a thought to you I can be sure that you receive it and respond to it.

Yes. How easily I get through to you, though, depends on how relaxed you are.

TWENTY-TWO
15 July

*I have immediate and spontaneous
manifestation of whatever I want*

> You said earlier that since you moved from the physical plane you have been continuing with your discussions and exploration. If it's okay with you, maybe you'd talk about how else you occupy yourself.

I loved walking when I was on earth. I made sure to fit in a walk every day if I could at all, Being with nature was very important to me and I experienced it in a profoundly feeling way. I still do all that.

Before I go further with your question I must explain that everything happens inside me first and then is manifested externally. Even putting it that way is misleading because it presupposes a linear progression. In fact, it's all simultaneous.

Now, once you understand that, you can see that I have immediate and spontaneous manifestation of whatever I want. So, I can walk through woodlands, sit beside streams, climb mountains, listen to birds singing, observe animals frolicking. I can have whatever type of house or apartment I want, or none at all, if that's what appeals to me. Nothing is fixed; all I have to do is wave my magic wand, as it were, except that I don't even need a wand. By mutual agreement I can be with whomever I wish. We can live together or separately or a combination of both, whatever suits us.

> On earth, intimacy between couples, including sexual intimacy, is a central driving force. If you don't think it an intrusive question, does that feature for you?

No question is intrusive as far as I'm concerned, so you needn't worry about that. I always have freedom of choice about answering.

I'll have to go into the question in some detail so that we agree on what we mean by intimacy, particularly sexual intimacy.

TWENTY-THREE
16 July

Intimacy: a level of communication between two or more which is totally free

Let's consider initially how intimacy works in your physical world.

For a start, I think it would be helpful if we concentrated on sexual intimacy. From the onset of puberty people begin to feel a need to express themselves sexually. What follows from that need may be multi-varied. Some may confine themselves to masturbation, which may be a form of intimacy with a person's own body. Some may seek external gratification through what you call one night stands, or brief encounters, which don't demand any depth of communication. (I'm excluding violent episodes, such as rape, from our consideration; I'm dealing with how people express their free will.) Some may feel a deep need for intimacy at what I might call soul level and may flit from one relationship to another looking for that. Some may decide to forego all sexual interaction until, they hope, a soul mate comes along.

A difficulty with sex in the physical state is that it may tend to be an obsessiveness trap. This can happen, for example, through promiscuity, or mandatory celibacy.

Now I think we need to broaden our exploration beyond sex in the sense of sexual relations. There's hardly any doubt but that all people need to share themselves in their innermost feelings and thoughts with special friends. It's self-evidently an extremely lonely existence for somebody to be cut off from all contact with fellow human beings. An extreme example may be solitary confinement in prison. O, yes, of course, there are exceptions, such as those who have deliberately chosen to be hermits, but they are still seeking intimacy by communion with their perception of the divine.

How may we attempt to define intimacy? I suggest: a level of communication between two or more which is totally free; in other words, where there are no inhibitions, no prejudices, no judgments, or, put another way, where they love each other unconditionally. Can we agree on that?

> Yes. Completely.

Now I go back to your question which was addressed to me personally. I don't have any sexual needs, i.e., for release, such as people on earth may be familiar with. If I wanted to, I could experience intimacy with another in a way which would be similar to two lovers enjoying sexual intercourse in their physical states. Bear in mind that everything that's possible on earth is also possible in spirit, but in ways that are indescribably easier and better.

> I notice that you say that, if you wanted to, you could. You don't say that you do.

I have to preserve some mystique! Anyway, all you need to know is the general picture.

Equally, of course, I have unlimited possibilities of intimacy with groups. And I'm not inclined to be a hermit. I never was, although I liked periods of withdrawal into my own space, as it were.

Have I answered your question to your satisfaction?

It looks like it's all I'm going to get anyway! Yes, you have. Thanks.

TWENTY-FOUR
17 July

The days of the bigots are numbered

If I can judge from what I've read of your writings and discussions, you didn't seem to be optimistic about people's relationships, with each other, and globally.

I was pointing out things that were obvious, like the negative effects of nationalism, religious prejudice, competitive practices, closed mindedness. All these things are still flourishing. You have only to observe how years of peace promoting efforts in a small province like Northern Ireland have continued to founder on the rock of entrenched positions. Every day your news media broadcast details of atrocities, all sorts of cruelties. If only people who perpetrate these barbarities would take a look at themselves in such a way that they would reach an understanding that what they're doing to others they're doing to themselves!

Nevertheless, I'm more optimistic now than I was in my physical state. All that's happening on earth is not so immediate for me now and I can take a broader view of it. I can see that there are more positively than negatively motivated people on earth at present. The days of the bigots are numbered.

TWENTY-FIVE
19 July

How to deal with money is a huge challenge for any soul embarking on a physical journey

Money, like sex, is one of the main preoccupations of people – perhaps the main one. Yet in spirit it apparently doesn't figure at all. That seems strange in the light of an often quoted dictum – "As above, so below".

On earth, on one level money means survival. The physical body has, generally, three basic needs – food, clothing, shelter. For these, money is the most common means of exchange.

On another level, money provides a gateway to luxuries of all kinds, to power, status, easily accessible sexual adventure, and so on.

On still another level, money is a motivation for all sorts of criminal activities, family feuds, obsessive behaviour in many directions.

Can you imagine what it's like for somebody who used his wealth to give him a position of advantage over others wherever he went when he discovers, after he exits his body, that even the humblest beggar has the same facilities as he has?

A fundamental distinction between living on earth and in spirit is that the physical body dies; in other words, the difference between a temporary state and (apparently!) an eternal one. Suppose we take an analogy of football, or cricket, or athletics, or any sport. Ambitious practitioners submit themselves to rigorous forms of training in order to reach as high a state of excellence as is possible for them. We might draw a parallel with life on earth. It's a game, but one intended to be played with the most serious of intentions, that is, to expand awareness. If we may use the word soul to describe the essence, the energy, that continues through whatever transitional forms it assumes, the soul ideally uses life on earth rather like an athlete uses a gymnasium or a practice arena. It comes up against all sorts of restrictive experiences that are designed to help it achieve internal freedom. The freedom it seeks is, of course, from habitual patterns of conditioning, all founded on, and reinforced by, fear. As long as it is controlled by fear it will never be able to express itself truly.

What has all that to do with money? Well, I suppose it's obvious that, as a powerful source of energy, it generates fear, through insecurity because of the lack of it, or manipulative practices by individuals or institutions in their use of it. It offers opportunities for people to be abusers or victims, or sometimes both. How to deal with money, then, is a huge challenge for any soul embarking on a physical voyage; and it's a challenge that the soul may or may not be familiar with depending on the extent of its experience of physicality.

Money couldn't figure in the same way in spirit as it does on earth because of the basic difference between how life operates in the two states. As we've already discussed, creativity has instantaneous manifestation in spirit. On earth, the physical element of doing intervenes so that time and linear progression enter the picture. Physical structures are created brick by brick, as it were; these include money and what it can buy. If there was immediate physical manifestation through imagination, without any need for doing, then, of course, there would be no need for money or any bartering system.

From all that you might be inclined to conclude that the saying –"As above, so below" – is inaccurate. In reality, though, it's not. That's because all creation, whether in spirit or on earth, happens from within. The existence of physical bodies, buildings, money, etc., tends to confuse the picture in so far as creation is concerned. Their existence is always temporary and, therefore, an illusion in the long run. That doesn't take at all from their importance as a means to an end – expansion of awareness.

> You made a point of not owning things, including money.

It could be argued that that was a form of opting out. From an early age I was sheltered from having to deal with material matters. But I generated a lot of money. I became an industry, if you like. And, mind you, I was industrious. In spite of my privileged position, I got caught up in the web of illusion that I've been talking so loftily about. Even though, as you said, I made a point of not owning things, I still got involved in sometimes acrimonious disputes to do with the industry that had grown up around me. I'm glad to be free of all that.

If people could rid themselves of fear, money would no longer play a centrally important role in their lives. The haves would share freely with the have nots and there would be plenty for everybody.

> My obvious question, then, is – how to get rid of fear?

I suggest that we leave that for consideration in our next session..

TWENTY-SIX
21 July

Is it possible to live without fear?

Is it possible to live without fear? In a physical environment it's very difficult. It can be argued that fear may be a necessary protection in certain situations, for example, in going alone into urban ghettoes, in being confronted by an armed robber, in avoiding punishment through being law abiding. Your world is full of potential occasions of fear – wars, muggings, rapes, bullying, intimidation, relationships, traffic, and so on. A person may wake up in the morning fearful of what might transpire during the day, and go to bed at night worrying about what happened during the day, or what may happen the next day. For somebody who's of a worrying disposition there's no end to fearful possibilities.

No matter how much we may go round and round with questions, the answers always come back to a simplicity – go within. In determining how to get rid of fear we don't have to go any further than that. When we find inner peace, an unbreachable inner security, then we are fearless, no longer susceptible to being controlled by fear.

You may protest that it's easy to say that but it doesn't solve the problem. I contend that it goes a long way towards solving it. If you're looking for inner security through some outside agency, like, say, money, property, lover, achievement, you're deluding yourself. All those have their value but you will never fully enjoy them if you are dependent on them.

I was using "you" in a general sense, but now, if you're willing, it may be helpful, in further exploring the challenge of fear, for us to be specific. Let's take you as a representative of the human species. Do you consider that you have found inner security and, if so, what constitutes it?

> To answer the first part of your question, I think I must say yes, I have, to a large extent. About time, I suppose! As to the second part of the question – what constitutes it – I don't find that so easy to answer. I'll have to tease it out, if you'll bear with me.
>
> My starting point was, probably, my acceptance that I'm a soul with a body rather than the other way round; that I'm an ageless infinite spirit being who happens to be on a human journey. In that acceptance I freed myself from fear of death as an end to existence, since there's no death, only a transition from one state to another.
>
> There was also, however, another fear associated with death which had to do with being judged by God and condemned to eternal punishment in Hell. (I wasn't too keen on the notion of Purgatory either.) That fear evaporated when my concept of God changed from that of an individual overseeing Presence to an energy, unconditional love, which is the essence of my being, as it is that of all souls, yet wonderfully adapted to each individual soul. Clearly, notions of eternal punishment and unconditional love were mutually exclusive – except whatever temporary hell I might create for myself; also out was any remaining shred of belief in the idea of a personalised deity sitting in judgment. Instead, I reached a state of unqualified acceptance that the ultimate destiny of all souls, without exception, is an infinitely blissful existence. As long as I can continue to

feel that, as well as accepting it intellectually, fear of what may happen, including worrying about people or situations, is dissipated.

I might add that having the privilege of communicating with you, and others who have also moved on, is a great help towards inner security.

I think it's only fair to say, too, that I trust completely in the unstinting help I receive from my guardian angels; help that is unobtrusive and non-directive, with a consequential bolstering effect on my feeling of inner security.

On radio this morning I heard a song with a refrain – "Ever since time nothing's been found that's stronger than love". In what was conveyed to me in one of my earlier books fear was described as an unaware expression of love. When I remind myself of that I find it easier to deal with any twinges of fear that intrude on my consciousness.

Well, that's a mouthful!

You asked for it.

Yes, indeed, I did, and thank you. That's your way and I acknowledge and respect its validity for you.

May I turn tables on you and ask you the same question you put to me?

I left you that opening, didn't I? Fear as a condition doesn't exist for me; in other words, I feel completely secure in myself.

The simplest answer I can give you as to what constitutes my inner security is I AM. A predictable answer, I'm sure, in the light of previous sessions. In saying I AM I'm also feeling I AM. That covers everything – me, my place in the universe, my interlinking with all life, my continuing, unfolding existence. In saying I AM I'm refusing to be defined; in fact, it's impossible for me to be defined because I'm infinitely unknown. That's my security, my peace, my freedom. I am as I am, spontaneous, unlimited, ever open to the unfolding joy and wonder of life. Thus I express myself fully, without fear; put more positively, with love, or, more accurately, in love.

> Is that it?

Yes, that's it.

> Since this is a book that, presumably, some people will read, I wonder how helpful what we've said will be to anybody who wants to know how to get rid of fear.

This isn't a ten easy steps to freedom book. Techniques are helpful if you want to learn how to drive a car or operate a computer, but they're a hindrance rather than a help where awareness is concerned. Each soul must find its own way. The best help we can give, in my view, is to share our experience, which we're doing by recording these discussions. Do you agree?

> Yes. It would be presumptuous of me to think otherwise.

And of me, too.

> If I may digress, is this book progressing to your satisfaction?

Yes. We had a somewhat "hands-off" start, but you're more comfortable with me now.

> Yes.

TWENTY-SEVEN

23 July

What is love?

I know that, earlier in our dialogue, you were somewhat reluctant to dwell on your life as J. Krishnamurti. However, having donned my fearless hat in the aftermath of our last session, I thought I'd ask you whether your reputation as Krishnaji matters to you now, bearing in mind how world wide that reputation was and still is.

May I congratulate you on having got up so early!

Thanks. (It's 5 a.m. He's teasing me – see his comments on 18 December last.)

I had better take advantage of this admirable enthusiasm on your part!

I wouldn't say that my reputation matters to me in the sense of it being important to me now, but it is relevant to the extent that these writings may carry more weight because of who I was. As I intimated earlier, I'm not interested in rewriting the records of my life. It was as it was.

What would you like to discuss on this bright morning?

I don't know. I'm completely blank.

Now that we've had a go at fear how about tackling love?

Fine by me.

Yesterday you quoted words in a song – "Ever since time nothing's been found that's stronger than love". That's true outside of time, too. Is love the absence of fear, or the transformation of fear? Is it enough to define it like that? In our last session I said that I express myself in love. I want to explore what I meant by that.

There are many tortured souls in your world – and mine; misery is not exclusive in its attractions, no matter the dimension. I'm aware of them and I want to help them to help themselves in any ways I can. However, I'm not a missionary and I realise that I can't "save" either world. I don't try to judge, nor do I see myself as superior to any soul. I accept all souls as they are and I respect their right to remain as they are, or not, as they wish. Is that love?

Suppose that there are some who say that I'm a fraud, a charlatan, that I set out to wreck people's beliefs. They may hate me and abuse me. All that doesn't affect my feelings for them. I respect their right to relate to me like that. Is that love?

Assume that I'm deeply attached to some individuals and I worry about them constantly in case something negative should happen to them. Is that love?

Let's say that there's one individual in particular with whom I long to be on the most intimate terms in an exclusive relationship. Is that love?

I could go on indefinitely presenting hypothetical situations that could all be regarded as love in action. We would, I suggest, at some stage come to the conclusion that there is nothing that love is not.

I'm going to surprise you by bringing into our consideration the notion of God as Creator, the Source of all being. In creating individual souls God gave them – us – free will, That gave us all carte blanche to go off and express ourselves in whatever ways we wished. I'm leaving out of our consideration that God is later on represented as having given us strict commandments as to how to behave ourselves in exercising our free will – which, in that event, obviously wouldn't be free will at all.

Let's take the notion of God a bit further. In some inexplicable way God remains in each of us even though we became uniquely individual. In giving us free will, then, God in us had, and has, so to speak, to put up with however we chose, and continue to choose, to express it.

In positing all that, can we now take a line on what love is? Can we say that it is that quality or essence that is totally accepting and places no conditions on that acceptance? Is that too limiting a definition? It is, isn't it? In an earlier session I indicated that I'd have no quibble with the notion of God if seen as unconditional love. But I have come to an impasse in seeking to understand what love is, although I can, perhaps, conclude that the word "unconditional" is tautological in that it's already implicit in the fullness of love.

> One of my other communicators, Shebaka, described love as *feeling and all its expressions*. In that context the word "unconditional" would have relevance, wouldn't it?

Yes. I like that description. It makes sense to me. It allows for an infinity of possibilities and it doesn't seek to confine the unknown – an impossibility, of course. You are somewhat surprised. Why?

> Perhaps more moved than surprised. You come across to me as so ... non-dogmatic and truly humble in your explorations.

You'll be putting a halo on me next if I'm not careful! But, thank you. Closed mindedness and awareness aren't compatible bedfellows.

TWENTY-EIGHT
24 July
Our reality in spirit is always a present one

Did you have any particular scheme in mind for this book? Did you want to make, say, X number of points?

You knew very well the answers to your questions when you were asking them. What else could my answer be but "no" to both questions? We're having a spontaneous dialogue, and if people would like to eavesdrop on it they're very welcome to do so – provided you go ahead with publication arrangements.

I may have to consult you about all that when the time comes. No doubt, from your lofty vantage point you'll be able to help the pieces fall into place.

I'm not asking you for details, but can you access the records of my other earth lives?

I can, if you want me to. That's the only basis on which I'd attempt to do so.

When you were on earth did you know about any of your other lives?

I had flashes, and, as you know, many pronouncements were made about me. In the early stages I was curious, but indifferent later.

> Are you still indifferent?

Let's say I found it interesting to do some research.

> How does that work for you? Would you see your different lives unfolding like, say, a movie?

No. That would put me back into time and linear progression dimensions. I can see and absorb the whole lot simultaneously. Our reality in spirit is always a present one.

> I suppose that's so also in the physical dimension – all my lives happening at once – although I don't think I can conceptualise that.

Physical happenings have to follow each other in a linear progression. That's the way your dimension works; brick by brick, if I may repeat that analogy. That's the hologram, the movies you've created. It's stored in the computer of your consciousness, where all the effects of the happenings have a present reality for you; thus you can conclude that all your lives are taking place at once. You can play the movie in a sequencing manner, if you want to. I stress the word "play" in the sense of diversion because, ideally, that's the way the whole operation will seem to you in due course.

Suppose we take the word "play" in its meaning of a stage production. You take on a role in it. While you're appearing in that role, you are, as it were, living the part, but still you know it's not real, don't you? A physical lifetime is an exact parallel. If people could only see it like that, they'd be saved a lot of aggravation.

> In that event they mightn't be inclined to take it seriously.

So? Don't you think your world would be vastly different if only people had that perspective? They could really enjoy themselves without getting all hot and bothered and killing and maiming each other over issues of no consequence.

The way we behave must seem utterly nonsensical to you. Of course. But, then, people are entitled to act out their roles in their own way.

TWENTY-NINE

25 July

Anything that's undertaken solely as a duty is not spiritually healthy

You talked a lot about meditation. Do you still meditate?

Yes. I'm sure your next question is – what do I mean by meditation?

Yes.

I'll start by telling you what I don't mean. For the purpose of this exercise I'll assume that I'm still in a physical body, so that I hope you can more easily relate to what I'm saying.

I don't mean a rigidly undertaken practice at a certain time and over a set period each day if such a practice becomes a duty or a pressure of any kind. Anything that's undertaken solely as a duty is not spiritually healthy.

It would be a mistake to see meditation and thinking as synonymous.

What's the purpose of meditation? In my view, it has to be to reach deeply into the inner being, the spring wells of I AM. It follows that meditation can't be an exercise leading to any specific conclusions, or, indeed, starting out with the object of arriving at such conclusions. If it has an aim, it is to still the traffic of thoughts and relax into the resultant void – which isn't, of course, a void in the sense of emptiness, but, rather, of freedom from all day to day worries and anxieties and pressures generally. The stillness allows a feeling of unity with all life – grass, flowers, trees, streams, rivers, animals, people, all that is.

It's a unity that's felt rather than thought about or analysed in any way. The feeling just flows through the meditation. To analyse is to seek to know; meditation, ideally, involves no effort.

> One of the most common difficulties that I have come across whenever meditation is discussed is how to stop the chatter of thoughts. What do you recommend?

One doesn't need to isolate oneself or set up a type of sanctuary in order to meditate. If these things help, of course that's fine. The main thing is to be comfortable.

As I said, meditation, ideally, involves no effort. Setting out to stop thinking presupposes effort, so it is important not to try to do so. If a thought comes in and you're trying to shut it out, you're actually strengthening it. If you leave it alone, just let it be, it will go away of its own accord. That's actually a worthwhile practice in itself – a non-doing, if you like, - irrespective of whether it's adopted as an aid to meditation or not, because it makes it easier for a person not to rush into judgment, which is the usual automatic reaction, born, as it is, of conditioning. Meditation practised without effort facilitates non-judgmentalism, without which there can be no freedom.

> Is meditation different for you now from how it was when you were on earth?

I'm outside of time, so I don't have to cope with the day to day pressures of living on earth, including the tiredness that's involved in that process. Consequently, thoughts don't clamour for attention in the same way as they would have tended to do in my human condition. But, when I reached a state of being able to move into the stillness beyond thought, I could transcend my human limitations and the process of meditation for me then was much the same as it is now.

THIRTY
27 July

The importance of experiencing each moment with no expectation from the next one

> I remember that in one of your books you made what I thought was a very interesting distinction between pleasure and joy; pleasure invariably brings pain in its wake, whereas joy has no restrictions.

I was using the word pleasure in the sense of an emotion created through an experience that the experiencer would wish to recapture in exactly the same way as in the original experience, which, inevitably, would prove to be impossible, with resultant pain. In other words, pleasure brings an expectation of repeat performance, whereas joy is spontaneous and carries no expectation of repetition.

People go on a holiday to a place where they have a marvellous time. They return a few years later with expectations based on their previous experience. This time everything's changed, they're miserable and they cut short their holiday.

Two lovers experiment during sexual intercourse with a position new to them and have a mutually wonderful time. They can hardly wait to try the same position again. When they do the experience falls far short of their expectations.

A man plays poker for the first time and wins a lot of money, much to his delight. In anticipation of a repeat performance he decides to try again and loses all he won, and more – a painful experience.

In using the words "pleasure" and "joy" in the way I did I was seeking to show how important it is to experience each moment with no expectation from the next one. As how you are in the present moment is influencing how you are in the next one, if you are spontaneously joyful in the present moment you are allowing yourself to be joyful in the next one, with no hooks on how you want it to be. Your experiences from moment to moment may, in fact, be entirely different from each other, but, since you're not trying to control them or steer them in any particular direction, you're not sitting in judgment on them by comparing them with each other.

> I imagine that it's much easier to be without expectation in spirit, where there's no time culture, than on earth, where there is.

Yes, it is, but the principle is the same. Even though the hands on your clocks keep moving forward, you can still only experience the present moment.

> I know, though, that I'm ageing with each moment and I expect that in X number of seconds, minutes, hours, days, weeks, months, or years I'm going to come to the end of my earthly life span. I'm aware that I'm acting out an illusory experience, but that doesn't take from its present reality. I have to plan ahead, to some extent at least, make appointments, if I need to travel somewhere I have to make arrangements, perhaps book accommodation, and so on. In order to be able to continue to exist in the physical world I have to project myself, as it were, into the future in some measure. And that's leaving aside looking forward with anticipation to some occasion that I would regard as having

special significance for me.

When you're doing all those things, your planning, anticipation, etc., you're still doing them from how you are in the present moment. So, while you are, in your terms, setting up future experiences, you're creating a vibration around them which boomerangs them back to you, so that, in a real sense, how they will be, again in your terms, is in alignment with how you are when you're setting them up. In other words, you're always operating outside of time although you think you're not because that's what your logical functioning seems to tell you.

How I am isn't static. Suppose I have just committed myself to a forthcoming event, say, to give a talk, which at the moment I make the commitment is something that I feel I'd love to do, and I'm looking forward to it eagerly. If I understand what you've been saying, that talk is now with me in my present moment of commitment and I'm setting up a joyful vibration around it. The talk is scheduled to take place four weeks from now. A week before the due date I'm beginning to get very nervous about it. I wake up during the night worrying about it. I'm certain that I have nothing worthwhile to say, I can't imagine how I'm going to keep an audience interested for ten minutes, let alone two hours, I'd withdraw from it but I'd be letting the organisers down; how could I ever have let myself in for this?

If we take everything as happening in the present moment, I accept the invitation to give the talk and I set up a joyfully positive vibration around it and I also set up an anxious negativity around it. (I'm leaving out of consideration the intervening three weeks since I'm outside of time.) How do I reconcile the two obviously contrasting states? And how is the talk affected?

I understand your dilemma. Logically, if all's happening in the present moment, you're giving the talk simultaneously with your acceptance of the invitation to do so. Clearly, that's not the actual position in so far as you are concerned. To complicate matters, your joyful state at the point of acceptance is transformed into an anxious one before the talk is due to take place. The facts are there and there's no fudging them with semantic gymnastics. But still I'm going to attempt to bring the two apparently irreconcilable positions together in a way that will be clear to you.

When you accept the invitation, the talk becomes a present reality for you. It's there in your consciousness in a positive way. It has a continuing present reality in your consciousness even as the vibration around it becomes negative. You are expressing your creativity through your talk. You are one with it and how you relate to it is a continuing expression of you. The fact that that relationship is changing is indicative of the spontaneity of your creativity. All has to be happening at once because your whole universe is in your present consciousness. Do I make myself clear?

> I suppose so. But the fact remains that if I give the talk while I'm in the joyful state of my acceptance of the invitation the mood and the substance and the audience's response to it are likely to be vastly different from the way they are if I give the talk while I'm in my negative mode.

Misunderstandings arise from trying to put things into words. When I say that all's happening at once, that statement may seem to imply that there's no evolution. The all that's happening at once is the all that's in your present consciousness – which is, in fact, all in every sense of the word as far as you are concerned – but your consciousness is always evolving, sometimes positively and sometimes, unfortunately, negatively. As I have already said, once you accept the invitation to give the talk it's in your consciousness as it continues to evolve. At the point at which you give outward expression to the talk how you express it is influenced by how you are in your evolving consciousness. Obviously, then, if you are constantly joyful in your consciousness you express in a joyful way whatever you choose to out of that consciousness. The obverse is also true, of course. Once the notion of the talk emerges into your consciousness it is there in a positive way and, as it evolves, also in a negative way. It's a mixed bag of ingredients, but, if your basic feeling about the talk is positive, that's likely to come across to your audience.

> Can a similar type of situation arise in spirit – for instance, in the discussions you hold, do they need to be organised in some way beforehand?

No, they are spontaneous happenings. It's as if, say, you turn on a radio or television set and you're immediately tuned in to a discussion with a phone in possibility of participating, if you so wish.

As I have said, things are easier in spirit. But, we all, whether on earth or in spirit, still operate through our present states of consciousness, and those of us who are on broadly similar wavelengths link up with each other when we are receptive to the broadcasts emanating from each other.

THIRTY-ONE
1 August
Whatever we create continues to live indefinitely

I realise that what we discussed in the last chapter was rather complex. Your use of the words "I'm not static" provides a key to clarity. If we were to say that all's happening at once and that's a static thing, then all would have already happened, if you see what I mean, and that would be finality, the END. The notion of all happening at once can only be understood, I suggest, in the context of evolving consciousness, which allows for ever expressing creativity; no stagnation, not for an instant. Does that help?

> Yes. On earth we're caught up with beginnings and endings, because that's the way things seem to be. A day ends, another begins. Seasons move into seasons and old years into new ones. Soon we'll be experiencing the end of a millennium and the start of a new one. Even in this book I'm putting in dates as we progress. The end of each chapter brings us on to a new date.

The book is a good example. Even though you have set it out in short chapters, which seems to you to be the best way to encourage the reader to stay with us, the material in each chapter is not limited by the words used, and each chapter evolves into the next, not necessarily in any linear way but in the sense of exploring questions that are relevant, or appear to us to be relevant, to the seeming mystery of life. Even when we reach a conclusion to the book it will continue to live on, certainly in your consciousness and mine, and also in some way in that of any readers. There's no end to anything because there's no end to us (as far as I know!). That means that whatever we create continues to live indefinitely —which could be an intimidating thought if we were into being judgmental. But we're not any longer, are we?!

THIRTY-TWO

9 September

Those who are open-minded find fellow travellers

The daily news bulletins reflect the divisions and entrenched positions throughout the physical world. Are there similar compartmentalisations in spirit?

Yes. The divisions are, in fact, more pronounced in spirit. People may be surprised to learn that mental barriers can often be more easily breached in your physical world than in spirit. That's because the dense physical vibration cloaks levels of awareness, with the result that there's interaction between the different levels in a much less obvious way than is usually the case in spirit. Ideally, that interaction provides opportunities for those whose conditioning has controlled their mindsets to let even chinks of openness through. One small chink is often enough to begin a process of questioning.

We have talked about the advantages of life in spirit, the freedom of movement, no financial or health problems, no ageing, and so on. What might be seen as a disadvantage by some is that there's no way to hide in spirit. I mean to hide what's going on inside. Suppose you meet somebody and you get into a discussion. The other person is expressing strong views about something. You might disagree totally with his views but you don't express your opinions, and he may even get the impression from you that you're agreeing with him. That couldn't happen in spirit. Our feelings and our thoughts are transparent.

Can you explain how that's so?

It's like the difference between darkness and light. Suppose you're sitting in a room in total darkness with somebody you've never met. You're completely unaware of each other's appearance, dress, etc. When the light is switched on you can see each other clearly. That's a rough analogy, but it may help you understand. Your physical body in its density creates a shroud of darkness around you, so that your light – what you call your aura – is obscured. When you leave your body the shroud is gone.

That could be very awkward, then, couldn't it? Say I meet somebody that I never liked, or with whom I was always uncomfortable, I can't cover up at all.

No. But what tends to happen is that you'll be drawn to a vibration that suits your mindset, so that you won't feel any need to cover up. Those with closed minds tend to be drawn together within the confines of their self-created prisons. Those who are open minded find fellow travellers. There's nothing to prevent interminglings of the two groupings except their own inclinations. As you can well imagine, the closed minded brigade aren't too likely to seek out the company of the others.

So, the state of mind I'm in when I move on will determine what grouping I'll gravitate towards.

Indeed. So you'd better keep an open mind! As long as you're not dogmatic about it, of course!

Would you say that there are more open minded souls than closed minded ones?

The balance is very much on the open side. The opposite is true of your physical world, but that's to be expected since the immediate purpose of its existence is to bring souls up against the restrictions they have placed on themselves.

> Are there many closed minded groupings in spirit? Is the rate of reduction in their numbers slow or fast?

A considerable number. Enough to keep the reincarnation shuttles moving for a long time, in your terms. The rate of reduction has accelerated, but it's still slow.

> Is there much slippage – I mean going back to old patterns?

That doesn't really happen. It may seem to in some instances, but in such cases the patterns of conditioning only pretended to be asleep for awhile. A certain amount of courage is needed to break away from what seem to be commonly accepted conventions or belief systems, and sometimes it's easier to give up and retreat to the seeming security of the herd. For most, though, when the break is made there's no going back. Take yourself, for example. You discarded all the religious traditions that were so much a part of your early life. Are you likely to have a deathbed conversion, or reversion, do you think?

> There's no likelihood of that. There were times, though, when I wondered was I deluding myself. Also, in writing the sort of books that I have been, and still am, questions troubled me about whether, for instance, I was responsible for leading others "astray". If only myself was involved, well, at least I could grin and bear whatever consequences might accrue.

I would hardly be the flavour of the month with any of your orthodox institutions. Yet, I'm here chatting away with you without a bother on me. Nobody has told me that I was a bad boy deserving severe punishment. Am I not living proof to you that you're not labouring under a delusion?

> Mostly you are. But, occasionally, doubts still surface. How can I ever really know for sure that you're on the other end

of the line, so to speak? I could be talking to myself all the time using a form of interior dialogue with a famous dead philosopher as a means of exploring metaphysical questions. The real Krishnaji, if he still exists, could be tearing his hair out, metaphorically speaking, observing a presumptuous charlatan putting words in his mouth, and, in the process, devaluing all his achievements during his long life on earth.

If that were so, or people thought it was, you could take credit for having developed a clever writing technique which would bring you kudos as a writer. Wouldn't that be something to be proud of?

No, it wouldn't; unless, of course, I acknowledged in an introduction to the book that I was using that sort of device. But I can't do that because I believe that that the one and only J. Krishnamurti is collaborating with me in writing this book and, indeed, initiated the project. In my wildest dreams I would never have presumed to do that.

Fair enough. But somebody could be impersonating K. You have read books written by people who sincerely believed that God was talking to them. How would you explain that?

I can't explain it if God is seen as a separate Supreme Being. But, if we're all God, as I believe, then it could be a genuine device for, say, an evolved soul to present teachings in a way that would carry weight with readers. Can you shed any light on the matter?

Let's concentrate first on whether I'm the genuine article or not. As far as I know(!), nobody is impersonating me – unless I'm fooling myself when I say that I AM. You'll have to take my word for it for now. Later on you'll know for sure. If you find that you have been deluded, you can keep out of the way of the real Krishnamurti!

I'll take my chances. Thanks for the reassurance.

You're welcome. As you have observed in the books you have read that have been written by different people who believed that God was talking directly to them, each God seemed to be vastly different from the others both in style and substance – that is, in how and what they presented. That's completely understandable if, as you believe, - and we have reached a level of agreement between us on this – God is in all souls and then, obviously, speaks in many voices. The device of God, as it were, speaking in one voice, that of the Supreme Being, could be seen as helpful (although I wouldn't agree that it is) in that it presents teachings in an authoritative way that's acceptable to those who are not yet ready to undertake the search for their own truth. That's in essence the same conclusion as you came to yourself.

A big difficulty with such a device, as I see it, is that it reinforces the notion of separation between God and souls, which seems to have been the source of all our troubles on our evolutionary journeys.

Well, you won't find me disagreeing with you, although I wouldn't put it quite like that.

How would you put it?

That sort of device is seeking to put clothes on what's better left naked. It's an attempt to identify the unknown in a personal way, which only spreads confusion in the long run, however helpful it might seem to be in the short term.

THIRTY-THREE
14 September

There's no difference in reality between the physical and non-physical states since reality is always internal

>We've been talking about living in the present, the continuing reality of it and all that. While realising that reality is always operating from within, one still can't ignore the fact that external conditions are continually subject to change. An obvious example is surely the difference between life in a physical body and out of it? As I'm writing this I can visualise you as I've seen you in photographs and on film. I can see you as a young man, middle aged and old. But, as you are now, how would I see you? The after image of the photographs is probably the best I can do while I'm still in the physical world, but, on the assumption that I'm not trying to keep out of your way, when I move on from here in what manner would we recognisably appear to each other?

In spirit, recognition is not a matter of appearance.

>But, in order to see each other, we'd have to take on some form, wouldn't we?

There are many souls here in spirit whom I knew when we were all on earth together. We recognise each other immediately without having to take on a form that would look like how we were in our physical bodies. We don't have to wear identifying badges, either!

But do you take on some form?

It's important to remember that, fundamentally, there's no difference in reality between the physical and non-physical states, since reality is always internal – in our feelings, thoughts and imagination, as we discussed earlier. When you're on earth you fit in with the modus operandi there; in other words, in order to be present on earth and to experience physical life, you need a physical body. On the other hand, I have abandoned my physical body or it abandoned me, whichever way you like to put it, and I'm fitting in with the way things are in spirit – I mean, of course, in an outward sense.

On earth, people's appearances change through, for instance, dress, makeup, hair styles, including loss of hair, plastic surgery, but mostly through the effects of passing years. Basically, though, the structure of the physical body, while it may expand or contract or grow wrinkled, etc., remains a physical identifier of you on your earth journey. However, that applies to one incarnation only. In all your other incarnations you chose different physical forms, some of them female. And that's not the whole story; your appearance before and between incarnations must be taken into account in our consideration of your questions.

To some extent it is so that how you are in yourself in your physical state is reflected in how you appear to other people. In spirit, it's always the case that how you are in yourself is reflected in how you appear to other souls.

You've asked me do I take on some form. I do. I'm not tied to any particular form. Your question isn't easy to answer in a way that will be understandable to you. Let's see how this works.

Suppose you have a huge wardrobe, filled with many different outfits. When you get up in the morning you select a particular outfit to wear, and you may decide to change it or part of it during the day. As a rough analogy, I draw a parallel between all the forms I have taken on – both physical and non-physical – throughout my evolution and all the outfits in your wardrobe. For instance, if I'm meeting souls who were with me in a specific lifetime, we can appear to each other as we were then. That, incidentally, can be a way to heal karmic patterns established during that lifetime.

> But, if you're in different vibrations, you're not likely to be meeting, according to what you said earlier.

That's so, but there are many whose evolutionary journeys have drawn them into similar vibrations.

Whatever form I take on is affected by how I am at present. For example, in some of my physical lives I was a rather obnoxious person. If, for some (most unlikely) reason, I chose to assume the outfit I wore – the body – in that life, it would be transformed in terms of countenance by my present state of awareness. So, in a sense, whatever form I use is an amalgamation of all the other forms that I have assumed during my evolutionary journeys into my present state of awareness. Can you follow all that?

> Yes, to some extent. I still find it difficult to visualise how, say, we might see each other when I leave my physical body.

If you want to, you can appear as you are now and I can appear as you recognise me through photographs.

The whole thing seems rather complicated when one tries to put words on it. But I assure you that it's utterly simple and can be great fun – like trying on different outfits from your wardrobe!

THIRTY-FOUR
21 September

How can there be a hierarchy in spirit if all souls are equal and each has free will?

Last weekend I was a guest speaker at an international conference where there were many references to Ascended Masters. Titles such as the Elohim, the Elim, Mahatma, Melchizedeck, Metatron, Maitreya, El Morya, Kuthumi, and many others, were in liberal usage, with the Elohim supposedly being the twenty-four nameless ones surrounding the Father Godhead.

In an earlier session we touched briefly on your public connection with the Masters before you moved away from all institutional frameworks.

The reason I bring this up with you now is that most of the people at the conference and at many similar happenings around the world seem to accept that there are all these hierarchies in spirit who are beaming down instructions to selected people on earth who are their agents in creating a new order, or way of being, on the planet; at least that's my understanding. I feel uncomfortable with the whole idea, which seems to me to promote a kind of robotic mindlessness, but, yet, I have to acknowledge that if the end result is peace and harmony on earth that can only be positive.

> If you don't mind, I'd be grateful for your comments (from your exalted heights of "Ascended Masterhood!").

I'll ignore that last remark! Are you asking me do all those Masters exist and is there really such a hierarchy in spirit?

> Yes.

You already know the answer to that. How can there be a hierarchy in spirit if all souls are equal and each has free will?

> Then, is all this stuff about Masters, etc., one big confidence trick?

Not necessarily. Remember we're not into making judgments. Game playing is not exclusive to earth. You're familiar with the stratagem of role playing used in training courses – and in healing therapies – in order to achieve a desired objective. The same type of thing happens in spirit. Many souls with the best of intentions are involved.

> But, when role playing is used in training courses, the participants know that what they're seeing is not real – it's just a type of drama constructed for their benefit.

Histrionic pageants have been used from time immemorial (in your terms) to create effects. For example, the Bible is littered with those sorts of devices. Many people like ritual and drama. Many like to be told how to live their lives. As long as what they hear and see and read is presented with emotionally inducing imagery and apparent omniscience they can happily surrender to what they believe is their greater good.

> Do you think it's their greater good?

As you know, it's not my way. Those who are the orchestrators – the so-called Masters, etc., - would argue that the road towards increasing awareness is built on stepping stones; in other words, people are spoon fed what they need according to their present levels of awareness.

> In your human state I think you'd have been more forthright in your comments.

Would I? Maybe I have mellowed. We all have free will. We can play whatever games we like. I came to the conclusion that the way I wanted to be, and for me it felt the best and only way, was to follow my own truth as it evolved and not to be controlled by anybody else's. This I continue to do to the best of my ability.

> According to what I have read, you were a devotee of the Masters for some time and you believed you were communicating with them and they with you. I know you've said already that that was part of your journey towards finding the freedom of your own way. I wonder is it intrusive to ask whether you were, in reality, communicating with them and they with you?

Nothing is intrusive, as I've already assured you. I wouldn't have called myself a devotee, but, yes, I did believe that evolved beings – Masters, if you like, - were communicating with me and I with them. You asked me, in an earlier session, whether I was a victim of delusion and I replied, no, I wasn't.

Perhaps I can clarify the whole situation for you this way. You get details of a course that offers you a way to enlightenment, or healing past traumas, or such like. You think that it might be a useful course for you to attend and you decide to participate in it. While you can see that many of the other participants are impressed by what's being presented during the course, you don't feel at all comfortable with it. When the course is over you realise that it wasn't what you were looking for; still, you're glad you attended it because it helped you to find your way, if only in terms of what you didn't want. Do you understand? It's as if there are many radio stations and many presenters sending out all sorts of broadcasts that are open to being tuned into according to a person's preferences or state of awareness at any given time. You find out what suits you – or what doesn't – by trying out different ones.

> What your broadcast is, if I'm correct, that, ultimately, the only station that will provide what we really need is based within ourselves.

Yes, indeed. I have played, and continue to play, that record over and over again. You understand, I hope, from what we've discussed in other sessions that I don't mean to imply, even to the slightest extent, that we can't be helped by tuning in to other stations – as long as we don't lose sight of the fact that we are, each and every one of us, in control of our own destiny. No matter what souls call themselves – Masters, or Avatars, or whatever, - if their message undermines that fact, or if they represent themselves as being superior to others, I would recommend leaving them to play their games with each other.

THIRTY-FIVE
27 September

Becoming ego-less

> In this sort of rambling dialogue that we're having, since we're not in the business of reaching conclusions, I wonder how much more do you feel should go into this book? In spirit terms there's a bit of a dilemma here, isn't there? We can't go on forever – at least I can't, in my present form anyway. What do you think?

Suppose we agree that you decide whenever you want to finish the book? That's only fair, since you're the one saddled with beginnings and endings.

> Agreed, thanks. Having the great privilege of communicating with you, I feel that I should have loads of questions. This morning I can't even think of one.

Are we moving, then, beyond questions? How do we continue to explore the unknown if we don't ask questions?

> Is there a state beyond questions?

Asking questions implies a thought process. We have already talked about the need for going beyond thought, from which follows going beyond questions. I don't want to be misunderstood, though; I don't mean to devalue thought. Conditioned thinking is the problem. When we're free of all prejudices, fixed beliefs, and so on, thought comes into its own. What we're aiming at is a total balance between feelings, thoughts and imagination to a stage where there's no longer any need to distinguish between them, where they're totally integrated. Then, you see, we're ready to question the unknown because we're no longer trying to fit it into any structure built upon circumscribed thought patterns.

> When we're here on earth there are always fairly obvious questions to be asked – although I couldn't think of one a few minutes ago. I imagine the most basic question is what happens to us when we die. If we accept that we continue to live on, we probably like to find out details about our new situation.

> You've been through all that and you're in a state of joyful being. You're continuing to have discussions, to explore the unknown. What does that mean? Can you give me an insight into what sort of matters you discuss?

In our first session I explained how I saw my role when I was on earth as Krishnamurti. Essentially, it was to help people find their own way, their own truth. That's what I continue to do. Because I'm not trying to influence anybody into conformity with my truth I have endless scope for enquiry into what souls see as their truths, and in the process I allow myself room for expansion of mine.

I don't want to give you an impression that I'm in a constant state of delving into deep, seemingly bottomless, wells of philosophical odysseys. I do when I feel like it. I exist spontaneously. As I said, I'm continuing to give help to those who need it in whatever ways I can. I do that, not because I have to, but because I want to. Call it the pull of unconditional love, if you like.

An interesting thing about existence in a non-physical state is that it's easier – once one reaches a certain level of awareness – to become ego-less; by that I don't mean any loss of individual identity – in fact, one becomes more whole as an individual. I'll use myself as an example.

From an early age in my last life on earth I was selected to be the so-called World Teacher, a type of Messiah. A world wide organisation was built up around me. People looked up to me, cherished every word I uttered, literally adored me, surrounded me with luxury. Of course I was flattered by all the attention and my ego blossomed. However, deep inside me I knew that all that wasn't what I wanted, so I walked away from it all. I didn't retreat into obscurity, though. I travelled the world, meeting, and talking to, thousands of people. I was still treated with respect and adulation wherever I went. I didn't seek any position of pre-eminence or status for myself, but it was automatically bestowed upon me. I have to be honest and admit that I got used to it and would have felt deprived without it, much as I tried to convince myself that I didn't need anything.

While I was on earth I aspired to be motivated, in how I was and what I did, without any trace of egotism. I succeeded to some extent, but not fully, as you'll have gathered from what I've already said. I'm not blaming myself for that. I would go so far as to say that it would be virtually impossible for anybody on earth with a publicly acclaimed profile to be totally free of egotism.

In spirit, though, it's as if I have retreated into obscurity. When I meet with fellow souls I'm not connecting with them as the "sage" Krishnamurti, but as I am, an expression of an ageless evolutionary process , as they are. From the standpoint of earth I'm no longer a tangible physical presence, so that how people relate to me through, for example, what they read is, as it were, put through a sieve of distance. It's more detached, as far as I'm concerned, with the result that my ego is not involved.

> However, if, say, people were constantly praying to you like they do with saints or prominent religious figures, or erecting statues of you, or continuing to venerate you in some way, would that boost your ego?

How could you ask me that?

> I don't mean you in particular. I'm hoping that you can answer in a general way. I wonder sometimes how does Jesus feel with so many millions of people praying to him and adoring him for centuries.

It wouldn't be appropriate for me to speculate on that. For myself, if my purpose was to spread a message of unconditional love, I wouldn't be too pleased by so many non-loving things being done in my name.

> You'd see yourself as a catalyst, perhaps, helping to bring to the surface subconscious negativities that needed to be dissipated?

Perhaps. But you were questioning me about whether my ego would be boosted. You can hardly be in any doubt about my answer.

> I take it that you like being ego-less?

Once it's clear that what you mean by ego is an unbalanced sense of one's own importance, a sort of arrogant superiority complex, yes, I do. That doesn't mean that I don't feel important. I do, but not more important than any other soul.

THIRTY-SIX
29 September
Unconditional love implies total freedom of being

Why do you feel important?

Because I am. I mean because I AM, not because I am important. The fact that I AM signifies that I have my own special place in the universal scheme of things, as you do, and every other soul does. So, of course, I am important. The wheels of the universe can't go round without me.

> We were discussing ego in the last chapter. It seems to me that there's a thin line between egotism and self-esteem. Lack of self-esteem is a hugely prevalent condition in the human state.

Not only in the human state. Because you're human at present it's understandable that your attention is focused primarily on that condition. Self-esteem doesn't pour down like a shower on any soul. It builds from within or not at all.

Do we understand what we mean by self-esteem? Holding the self in high regard? Respecting one's own value? Without an inferiority complex of any kind? Loving oneself unconditionally? What do you think?

> I would imagine that the last one – loving oneself unconditionally – is all-embracing.

Is it easier to love others unconditionally than yourself?

> The inner critic tends to be nourished from very early in our lives by all sorts of external agencies – family, school, peer groups, etc. – with the result that we are continually watching ourselves in action and don't easily let go of controlling tendencies.
>
> I think the answer to your question is that the two things are intertwined. The more I love myself unconditionally, the easier it is for me to love others in the same way. So, as I expect you would say, all answers come from within.

That's the simplicity of life. If we hold on to that we don't need to get all hot and bothered about external factors. When we love ourselves unconditionally, that love flows around all those with whom we are in contact and spreads out into the universe as a whole. Once we love ourselves unconditionally, it is impossible for us not to love all others similarly.

> In my experience, some people feel intimidated by the notion of unconditional love. They might say that the theory is fine, but putting it into practice is a different story. An obvious example is that of a woman who is raped. How can she bring herself to love unconditionally the man who so brutally assaulted her?

When I say that I love myself unconditionally, I mean that I accept myself as I am. I'm not excluding the possibility, even the probability, that I might not like how, or aspects of how, I express myself; in other words I leave plenty of scope for improvement in how I feel about myself.

In the case of the female victim, it's putting it mildly to say that she didn't like how her abuser expressed himself. It would be asking too much to expect otherwise of her, and to do so would, in fact, be a misunderstanding of unconditional love. In her case, how I see her expressing unconditional love in the immediate aftermath of the abuse is like this: acceptance of herself as she is (perhaps feeling angry, bitter, humiliated, violated, generally disturbed), and also acceptance of her abuser as how he is (perhaps brutish, sadistic, violent, misogynistic). As her life evolves, she comes to realise that it's self-destructive for her to allow herself to continue feeling victimised, and she releases all the negative emotions that have been caging the joy in her. In the process, she also frees herself from the control that her abuser has continued to exercise over her while she remains emotionally connected to the rape. She accepts him in his unawareness and lets him go.

Releasing all the negative emotions is a huge step, isn't it?

Yes. Unconditional love understands that. It embraces all the negatives as well as the positives. It makes no demands. In its fullness it is virtually an unattainable objective in the human condition. The main thing is to be attuned to it, to want to be it.

A perception of unconditional love may be that it's a sort of kill-joy thing – like, for example, not feeling free to gossip anymore. I don't mean malicious gossip.

Unconditional love implies total freedom of being. It also, of course, involves accepting and allowing that for every other soul. In that realisation, what harm is there in indulging in occasional gossip?

THIRTY-SEVEN
9 October
If you are yourself you cannot fail

> You travelled the world giving talks to often very large audiences. How did you prepare for your talks? To what extent did you use the same format with different audiences? How did you know whether your listeners were connecting with what you were saying? Did you suffer from nerves before you were due to give a talk?

I prepared in silence. I went into a void, so to speak. Out of that void emerged what would form the basis for my talk. Of course I repeated myself over and over again, but never word for word, because I delivered each talk spontaneously. I didn't concern myself unduly with whether I was connecting with my listeners or not. Each of them would hear me in his or her own way. As long as people kept turning up to listen to me I felt that it was fair to assume that they were interested in what I had to say.

Did I suffer from nerves before a talk? In the early stages, yes, particularly when I was, as it were, the band leader. Once I settled into the role I had chosen for myself – or, more accurately, once I had decided to be myself – I prepared assiduously through rest and meditation and trusted that whatever words I needed during the course of a talk or discussion would come to me. I was in a state of total attention.

Have I answered your questions to your satisfaction?

You have been very helpful, thanks.

A useful thing to remember is that, if you are yourself in whatever situation you may find yourself, you cannot fail. You may well ask how can you be anything but yourself. Once you're controlled by fear it's impossible for you to express the true you. Fearlessness is the key to success.

Which brings up the obvious question: what do you mean by success?

And I'll give you the obvious answer: being yourself.

THIRTY-EIGHT
3 November
Spontaneity is just being

Welcome back. What would you like to discuss today?

> I don't know. I'm hoping that you'll come up with something.

Do you think that I'm aware of everything that's going on in your life?

> I suppose you could be if you wished. I hadn't imagined that you'd be continually looking over my shoulder. I'd expect you to have much more interesting and enlightening things to do than that.

Actually, unless you invite me to, I don't seek to link up with whatever is happening for you. I wouldn't want to invade your privacy in any way. If you feel that I can help in any of your activities, I respond gladly to the best of my ability.

> Thanks. I'll remember that.

> In the context of discussions I'm having with different groups I have been thinking about spontaneity and whether, in fact, adults ever act without having reasons to do so. Even if I go for a walk, for example, am I doing that because it's good for me, that I need the exercise, etc? Once a child starts to use its reasoning faculties, does that spell, if not the

end to, at least a limitation on, its spontaneity?

Are you implying that it's a negative thing if you have a reason for all your actions?

Not necessarily, although I think it would be nice if I could be totally spontaneous sometimes.

Feelings are spontaneous before thoughts get to them, or before people are conditioned to allow analytical processes to take over control of their lives.

You look out a window. You haven't any particular reason for doing that. You're not trying to see anything specific. You just happen to be facing the window. You see grass, or flowers, or walls, or trees, or the sky, or the whole lot together in a sweeping glance. You have a nice feeling about whatever you see. It's something that registers with you. You don't need to think about it, to analyse it. That's spontaneity, isn't it?

Yes. In a passive way.

In a creative way, I would say.

I mean that it's not active in the sense of doing something.

Is seeing – looking – not doing?

Yes, of course. But what I'm trying to explore is more the physical follow up to a spontaneous feeling. I don't mean lashing out in anger or something like that, which results from an unbalanced emotional charge rather than a spontaneous upsurge of feeling that happens for no apparent reason.

Isn't spontaneity just being? Does doing have to come into the equation at all? Or, if it does, is that relevant? Perhaps the being and the doing can merge into each other, with feeling, thought and imagination totally in harmony, as we discussed in an earlier session.

THIRTY-NINE
24 December

I see an increasingly stimulating planet where most people will be drawn to love, rather than maim and kill, each other

Here on earth we're embarking on a new millennium. Does that mean anything to you?

No. It's of no consequence whatever as far as I'm concerned.

Some people believed that the planet would have been obliterated by now. All sorts of dire predictions had been made about the end of the world and other almost equally armageddonish types of catastrophes. While there were, as always, localised disasters, such as earthquakes and floods, there was no global cataclysm. Symbolically, I suppose, the predictions could be seen as heralding new happenings, changing consciousness, and so on, although they weren't expressed in that way. Perhaps you have some comments to make on all that?

In saying that the new millennium is of no consequence to me I'm referring to me as I am in a spirit state, which is outside of time, so that I'm no longer conscious of time, as you are, in terms of days, weeks, months, years, etc. But, as a fairly recent emigrant, in your terms, from the planet, I am still very much in tune with physical happenings. And since, after my fashion, I did my best over a long number of years to help people find their truths, I want to continue to stay in touch with developments on earth and to be of assistance where I can.

Celebration, whatever brings joy, is always helpful. Observe how nature celebrates. You'll soon be moving into spring with all its spontaneity of blossoming beauty. It is good to bear in mind the effortless example of the changing seasons.

Solutions to all problems, both individual and global, lie within each person. You are expressing your truth on a continuing basis through your feelings, thoughts and imagination, (and so is every other person on the planet similarly expressing his/her truth). That truth not alone shapes your destiny but has a profound effect on global consciousness in ways that you couldn't even begin to conceptualise. (Again, what I'm saying applies to each individual.) When, then, there's a happening such as the beginning of a new millennium it brings an opportunity for people to unite in a hope-filled, joyful, welcoming of the present and a letting go of the divisiveness of the past. Ideally, the positive effect is astronomical.

Conditioning, through past experience, tends to influence people towards pessimism. Repeated rejections and disappointments don't provide a steady platform for optimism. The pessimistic trend is reflected in predictions such as those you mentioned. People united in pessimism are equally as influential as those united in optimism.

The fact that there were no cataclysmic happenings, such as the elimination of the planet, should provide reassurance that movement of consciousness through the twentieth century has been, at least marginally, on the side of the angels, so to speak. A note of hope, wouldn't you agree?

> Yes, indeed. Although a lot of predictions were made about you, you didn't get involved in that field yourself, did you?

I was influenced by them in the early part of my life. In particular, I had received assurances about my brother's health which turned out to be false. That was a disillusioning experience for me at the time. On the plus side, though, I came to realise that how I lived each moment created my future – or, more accurately, my continuing present. I'm not a killjoy. I know a lot of people like getting predictions. The reservation I would have about that is the self-fulfilling aspect of it, particularly where negative predictions are concerned. If predictions help to increase people's awareness of their potential, their untapped creativity, then I'm all in favour of them. People need to be continually encouraged not to allow themselves to be caged in by conditioned perceptions of their abilities. Almost invariably, risks are involved in undertaking new ventures, or in changing existing patterns of existence, which, although limiting, have an adhesive perception of security. That's part of the adventure of life and highlights the value of the earth experience as a vehicle for shifts in consciousness.

> May I now take a risk and ask how you see life on earth evolving?

I am much more hopeful than I was when I was on earth. Your daily news bulletins bombard people with details of atrocities, and such like, committed in different parts of the world. The marvellous advances in the technology of communication have enabled this to happen; and it's good that the shadowy side of how people treat each other is no longer easily hidden. The downside is that the heavy emphasis on what I might call the minus side of life facilitates an impression of a world with a plus deficiency. If people see it that way, what emanates from them is likely to be negatively focused, with a resulting damaging effect on global consciousness. The message that I would like to convey is that more and more people are accepting the challenge of freedom from the controlling influences that imprisoned past generations. I see an increasingly stimulating planet where most people will be drawn to love, rather than hate and kill, each other.

FORTY
9 February 2000
Being open to possibilities

You have been wondering whether my comments at the end of our last session would be an appropriate conclusion to this book. Well, as I've already said, that's up to you.

> During the past two days I sat and waited for some time but I couldn't get any sense of you at all. So I thought that maybe we had reached the end of the line.

You needed rest. I'm a demanding communicator. Bridging the gap between our worlds isn't easy. However, there can be a big advantage from a communication standpoint in dialogue between human and spirit beings in that it is potentially very pure. In inter-human conversation words are usually used indiscriminately and what's intended to be conveyed is liable to degrees of distortion. Because I'm not using words in my communication with you, you're reaching into me in a way that you wouldn't normally achieve in your dialogue with fellow humans. That involves intense attention on your part.

> And, I presume, a lot of patience at your end.

Understanding, maybe, more than patience. It's a most useful experiment from my point of view. As you know, I loved words – still do. But now I have to be content with whatever words you choose to put on our communication. That's our agreement.

You have your style and I fully understand that you wish to present whatever we discuss in a way that you consider will be easy to read. You aren't happy that that was the case with a lot of my published material.

> That's only my opinion. It's just that, I suppose, I'm more comfortable with my own form of expression. I don't mean that as any judgment on yours – unless you would regard admiration for the scope and originality of your thinking in that light.

You don't need to explain. I understand. My point is that, in my projecting at you whatever I want to communicate and in you putting that through your processes of understanding and language capacity, we have a good chance of eliminating the haphazard quality inherent in what might be called day to day conversation.

> Isn't there also the possibility, though, that I might completely misinterpret what you're conveying to me?

I'm not likely to let you get away with that! If I feel that you haven't captured the sense of what I'm attempting to convey in any segment of our dialogue I have no difficulty in getting through to you about that.

> Would you say that it's a good idea for people to leave themselves open to communication from spirit sources?

Look at how people are communicating with each other at present through, for example, the internet. Once somebody accepted the possibility of such a development, that allowed it to happen. What usually prevents development in any field is closed mindedness, or vested interests in maintaining the status quo. If you weren't open to the possibility of our communication we wouldn't be cooperating on this book.

> The idea of widespread conscious communication between

the human and spirit states embraces acceptance of continuing life and, even where there is such acceptance, freedom from fear of what is regarded as "paranormal".

I'm only talking about being open to possibilities, not probabilities or certainties. Fear is the big bugbear. Where there's no fear anything is possible.

Do you foresee a stage when human and non-human beings will be able to communicate with each other at will – like people are doing now with each other?

Yes. It's inevitable.

Are you in favour of that sort of development?

I'm in favour of anything that helps people to free themselves from fear.

FORTY-ONE
11 February
Where there's no fear there's no risk

> When you were on earth did you feel that you were doing all that you wanted to do with your life?

Eventually, yes. Not in the early years, as we've already discussed.

> In my experience, people have huge problems not knowing what they'd like to do, even if they were free of economic pressures; and, if they could determine that to their satisfaction, how they could arrange it.

Fear rears its ugly head again. People let themselves drift into situations and then become controlled by the situations. Duties and responsibilities take precedence over the joy of creative expression.

> Suppose we take an example of a man and a woman who marry and have children. They have experienced one form of joyfully creative expression through having children. However, they find no fulfilment in their careers, but feel that they have no choice but to stay with them in order to provide comfortable upbringing and suitable career opportunities for their children. They are not complaining. They make the sacrifice because it's what they want to do on their children's behalf. But, when the children have become

adults, the parents are still relatively young, with little or no change in their perception of their careers. They feel that it's now too late for them to make any radical moves; it would be difficult for them to adjust, they would probably have to settle for reduced incomes, they might lose pension entitlements, etc. What's in store for them may be to fade into retirement and old age.

That's probably a typical example of duties and responsibilities, albeit gladly borne, taking precedence over the continuing joy of creative expression. How would you get round that sort of situation?

Ideally, when people have children, they love, and care for, them. But sacrificing their lives for them is of no use either to the children or themselves. In any case, their inevitable frustration at the lack of fulfilment in their careers will communicate itself to the children and will most likely have negative effects on them.

From an early age some people have strong feelings about what they'd like to do with their lives. I would suggest that most people have clear preferences about what they don't want to do. All educational establishments need to have guidance facilities where individual talents can be explored, with extensive opportunities for experimentation.

The situation that you have outlined is a clear-cut example of the effects of conditioning. Why should an either/or syndrome be present? What's to stop the couple in question from exploring what they'd like to do and then going ahead and doing it? I know – you have already dwelt on some of the considerations that would influence them against taking such apparently radical action. Those considerations have no real validity. I was never an advocate of martyrdom, much less now.

Is what you're saying that people should never confine

themselves in situations where they have no outlets for creative expression?

I'm not into "should" or "shouldn't" pronouncements. If they want to make the best possible use of their time on earth, the answer is obvious.

Take a risk?

Where there's no fear there's no risk.

FORTY-TWO
29 February

If there's one legacy I'd like to give people it is that they would no longer be controlled, even to the slightest extent, by fear

> In recording our discussions, spread out, as they have been, since October 1998, I haven't been conscious of, nor indeed particularly interested in whether there is, any linking theme running through them. However, on a re-reading it strikes me that there's a recurring emphasis on the destructive power of fear. Accordingly, I thought a suitable title for the book might be *Living Without Fear*. What do you think?

I agree wholeheartedly. If there's one legacy I'd like to give people it is that they would no longer be controlled, even to the slightest extent, by fear. It might be argued that a more positive title would be *Living With Love*, or something similar. However, I would prefer to place emphasis on taking fear out of the equation; once that's achieved, love is no longer caged and can express itself totally, without restriction, which is what it's always striving to do.

> I feel that it's time to bring the book to a close. I hope that's not short changing you. It's a short book, and I'm sure that you have lots more enlightening and inspiring insights that could desirably be included. Is it okay with you if we call it a day?

Yes. We have engaged in a little exercise in exploration that I hope people will find helpful. As I have already intimated, it has been a useful experiment for me.

> We're finishing on the pivotal day of the first leap year of the new millennium. A small leap or a giant step, maybe.

That's up to you. It can be a giant leap, if you so wish.

> I'm deeply grateful to you for having chosen to communicate with me and also for your patience with my slowness in grasping what you were transmitting.

We have to cope with different dimensions – which is, at least, an effective cure for any tendency towards long-windedness! My thanks to you for agreeing to chat with me.

> Would it have made for more flowing communication if, say, I could have gone into trance and you could have spoken through me?

That wouldn't have been much of an experiment as far as I'm concerned; nor, indeed, would it seem to me to be a progressive way towards breaking down the barriers between the different dimensions. I think it's important that, since our dialogue is presented in a physical form, it should be filtered through the human agent's thoughts and language construction.

> I'll resume contact with you, I hope – in whatever dimension!

It's your choice. As I told you, I'm glad to help if ever you want to call on me.

> Does that apply to our readers?

Of course. It applies without restriction. Readers or non-readers, all are welcome. Except that I don't want anybody praying to me; just ask, that's all. I'll help as best I can.

EPILOGUE
20 June

I have recently read *The Inner Life Of Krishnamurti* by Aryel Sanat, published in 1999 by Quest Books. It's a fascinating book and I'm delighted to have found it. However, as a result of reading it, I feel I need to go back to K for some clarification.

I think it's fair to say that a commonly held public perception of K's life and work is that, while there could be conflicting explanations for his reported association as a boy and young man with the so called Masters, with much speculation tending towards his having been a victim of delusion, once he disbanded the organisation built up around him any connection he may have had with the Masters, delusional or otherwise, ceased. Aryel Sanat discounts that perception. His thesis is that K's association with the Masters, particularly the Lord Maitreya, continued on a daily basis throughout his life. He adduces evidence to support that thesis from comments made by K during occasional private discussions.

In some of my sessions with K recorded in this book we discussed his connection with the Masters. He didn't deny the existence of the Masters or the validity of his early experience with them, but he made no mention of life long communication with them. I didn't ask him about that, of course. I'm doing so now, and I'm waiting for a response, hoping that he's still available to answer my call.

I'm always only a thought away, as I told you. Who do you think guided you to that book?

Something radical needed to be done to free people from their subservience to icons and organisations, to help them to express their own unique individuality. As the head of a world wide organisation I would have perpetuated that which I came to end had I continued in the role that was expected of me. At the same time, the public profile that I had acquired through the organisation was a considerable help to me when I set out on my teaching mission. My opposition to organisations was given flesh and blood, so to speak, by my having been head of such a body and by having disbanded it, with the consequential loss of all its attendant status and security. You might say that all was as it was meant to be.

If I had publicly proclaimed that I was a channel for the Lord Maitreya, or some such exalted sounding being, I'd have focused attention on me as somebody with special supernatural powers, which would have completely undermined what I was attempting to achieve, involving helping people to realise that there are no greaters or lessers, that each individual is uniquely special.

Look at the history of human evolution. Running right through it is a recurring theme of enslavement of people. This has happened through abuse of power, by some setting themselves above others, and so on, but, ironically, it has also happened through individuals and organisations whose stated purpose was to help people find salvation. How could I effect change if I was part of all that?

I needed to present myself as one individual, free of all institutional trappings, asking questions and seeking answers from within. I hoped my example would encourage others to do likewise.

You will recall that in some of our sessions we talked about the help available from spirit guides. I'm enthusiastic about that provided it's accepted as a self empowering thing. It would be foolishly egotistical of me to pretend that I wasn't helped by spirit guides on a continuing basis during my life as K. Of course I was. I readily admit that I couldn't have managed without that help. I also readily admit that my helpers were (are) evolved souls. I don't like the term "Masters" because of its hierarchical connotations, but as a word I suppose it's as good as any other one.

> I'm somewhat surprised by your admissions. I'm delighted and affirmed by them since all my experience has made me a public proclaimer of my constant need for help and the readiness with which it's given by guardian angels/spirit guides – much more appealing conceptual terminology to me than Masters. I don't see, though, how acknowledgment of that sort of help would have been in conflict with the notion of self empowerment. It would have enhanced it, I'd have thought.

As you know, for the greater part of the twentieth century (and in earlier centuries, of course) people were conditioned to authoritarianism. They looked to those whom they perceived as higher authorities for answers, to be told what to do. Masters, or similarly designated hierarchical figures, fitted easily into that sort of configuration and people would have continued to be entrenched in their conditioned ways of thinking and obeying orders "from above" unless something radical was done to upset that pattern. I was aiming to help people to strip away the bonds of slavery and to be free, which, incidentally, meant being free of all "Masters". Once they reached that state they would be able to see themselves as receiving help on an equal to equal basis rather than directions from superiors to inferiors.

> If all the traditional sources of help were discarded, from where would help come? Is there a risk in promulgating self dependence as the be all and end all that a person would feel totally isolated?

That's not my purpose, nor was it ever. All forms of class perceptions, in spiritual as well as material cultures, needed (and continue to need) to be eliminated. That meant, and means, no concept of superior and inferior. It was the view of my helpers and myself, taking into account the prevailing states of consciousness at the time I embarked on my mission, that, in order to help people towards increased confidence in themselves and greater self esteem and to reduce and, ideally, eliminate their dependence on authority figures, it was desirable that I would not be perceived to be in constant communication with "Masters", with the implication that I was merely acting as a voice for them and/or taking orders from them.

I had been portrayed as a vessel for the Lord Maitreya. If that was my public image, how could I have presented myself as a free man, or with what credibility could I have encouraged others to set themselves free?

Incidentally, I was never an automaton, a mindless conduit of ideas, etc. I accepted help as an equal amongst equals, irrespective of whether help came from physical or spirit sources.

> If it is a fact that all this is not a figment of my imagination and that you, K, are truly communicating with me, is there a risk that revealing yourself as you are doing now will adversely affect the perceived validity of your teachings?

How could it? I see all that we have discussed in our sessions as reinforcement of my earlier teachings. I have expanded them somewhat, that's all.

> In your public pronouncements, though, you were strongly opposed, without qualification, to dabbling in occult experience.

I still am. Let's be clear about what we're discussing. For many people such dabbling becomes a diversion, a search for spurious excitement or a quick fix, like seeking out so called gurus to release karma in the foolish belief that such people have the power to do so. There's hardly much advantage in substituting a spiritual class system for a physical one.

> But where does that leave us? Couldn't what we're doing be regarded as dabbling in the occult? And people would, understandably, think so.

In an earlier session I drew attention to the importance of us relating to each other as equals. We're both spirit beings. The only difference is that I'm in one dimension and you're in another. I don't want people to see our communication as, essentially, any different from, say, you having a telephone conversation with a friend in America. I want to take away all the mystique, the ritualistic contortions and pietistic outpourings that prevent people from being themselves.

What does occult mean to you?

> I have looked up my dictionary. Definitions include "kept secret, hidden, involving the supernatural, mysterious, beyond the range of human knowledge".

Do you think our discussions are covered by those definitions?

> They might be regarded as involving the supernatural. They could hardly be seen as falling within the range of common, everyday, human experience.

Not yet. Isn't it fair to say that what we're at is helping people to open doors to themselves, to let them see that nothing is hidden and that there is no cache of secret knowledge to which they are not entitled to have access?.

Have I set your mind at rest?

    Yes. I am most grateful.